Praise for *Student-Led Assessment: Pro...* *and Achievement Through Portfolios and...*

Student-Led Assessment is quite literally the book I knew I needed and could never find in a single volume. Sackstein seamlessly integrates proven teaching practices, common sense, and student-centered approaches to provide the essential resource for teachers of any level and any background. I keep it with me whenever I am coaching educators on the sound principles of standards-driven teaching and learning, and I have found it an invaluable guide for collaborative conversations that drive improvements to practice in relevant and practical ways. Prepare yourself—once you start reading, you won't be able to put it down!

— **Dr. Lindsay Prendergast**, school improvement coach, NWEA; producer, Educators Without Borders; framework specialist, The Danielson Group

Transitioning to anything outside a traditional grading system is a mindset shift as well as a heavy organizational lift. In the work that I have been completing with my own district, there has been much trial and error because no one has put together a resource to support the work quite like this. Starr's newest book captures the process of transitioning to a portfolio lens for students and teachers. She does it in a way that is nonthreatening and works to educate while changing mindsets. This is a resource that teachers and school leaders can use to facilitate their own grading transformations to a portfolio-based assessment system. I wish I had access to a resource like this, vignettes and all, when I started this work.

— **Katie Harrison**, educator and grading reformer

This book is simply a breath of fresh air, offering a practical roadmap for educators to turn the ideals of student assessment capability into a daily classroom reality. Authored by a seasoned educator and assessment expert, this book takes a bold step beyond mere rhetoric and generalized academic research, providing tangible strategies and actionable insights across the school year to support teachers in ensuring that empowerment becomes a daily reality for all students.

— **Michael McDowell, EdD**

Starr Sackstein does it again in this probing and thought-provoking guide to student-led assessment for today's dynamic educators and leaders. She leads readers through a poignant reflection about why and how we engage in assessment practices in the classroom that is relevant to today's demands, rich with examples, and highly accessible. Starr provides practical, turn-key approaches to enriching classroom dialogue and assessment with student voice that are inclusive and grounded in critical relationship development for teachers and students. Truly a must-read!

—**Dr. Alexandra Laing**, 2022 ASCD Champion in Education; founder and principal consultant at New Edge Leadership; coauthor of *Climate Change Education*; senior research officer at the University of the District of Columbia

If you're looking for practical and tangible methods that position students at the center of their own learning, Starr Sackstein is your best source and mentor. *Student-Led Assessment* will walk you through the shifts necessary to embrace a culture of student self-assessment, awareness, and reflection. She tackles the challenges of when and how to conference with students and shares structures and protocols to apply immediately to engage students in metacognitive and honest dialogue. As we prepare students to be complex thinkers and lovers of learning who develop learning dispositions, Sackstein is just the assessment expert that everyone needs in their ear.

—**Connie Hamilton**, author, educator, speaker, and presenter

As the title of this book indicates, author and veteran teacher Starr Sackstein shares her experience and expertise in engaging students in the deeply meaningful and transformative work of self-assessment. Throughout the chapters, Starr weaves examples and stories that illuminate the humanizing process of students developing autonomy and efficacy in leading and evaluating their own learning. While the stories are inspiring, this book also offers valuable, practical resources and structures to truly support teachers in implementing student-led assessment in their classrooms. I highly recommend this book as an indispensable guide to fostering a learner-centered culture.

—**Abigail French**, CTE pathways coach, Frederick County Public Schools, Winchester, VA

For many years I have advocated for creating a culture of learning, not a culture of grading, in our classrooms and schools. In this book, both comprehensively and practically, Starr Sackstein provides the building blocks for a culture of learning and for students developing as capable, reflective, independent learners. In particular, the chapters on developing a portfolio system and using student-led portfolio conferences instead of parent-teacher conferences provide teachers with the thinking and processes they need to implement the critical components of classrooms and schools that focus on learning and students' ownership of their learning. I wish that I had had this book when I was in the classroom because using it would have made me a better teacher, and my students would have learned more and developed better as learners.

—**Ken O'Connor**, author and consultant, Assess for Success Consulting

Putting students in charge of their learning with student-led assessment is a game changer! Starr's firsthand expertise and experience working with diverse educators make portfolios and conferences both accessible and possible for educators at all levels. This book should be a staple in all schools to support these needed shifts in assessment!

—**Katie Martin**, cofounder and chief impact officer, Learner-Centered Collaborative and author of *Learner-Centered Innovation* and *Evolving Education*

In *Student-Led Assessment*, Starr Sackstein provides the context for implementing learner-centered practices that promote a classroom culture of assessment driving students' investment in their own learning. This practical guide is a how-to manual for teachers committed to making the shift in their instructional and assessment practices.

—**Walter McKenzie**, author of *Intelligence Quest: Project-Based Learning and Multiple Intelligences*

Student-Led Assessment

Also by Starr Sackstein

*Assessing with Respect: Everyday Practices That Meet
Students' Social and Emotional Needs*

*Peer Feedback in the Classroom: Empowering Students
to Be the Experts*

*Teaching Students to Self-Assess: How do I help students
reflect and grow as learners?* (ASCD Arias)

Student-Led Assessment

Promoting Agency and Achievement Through
Portfolios and Conferences

Starr Sackstein

Arlington, Virginia USA

2800 Shirlington Road, Suite 1001 • Arlington, VA 22206 USA
Phone: 800-933-2723 or 703-578-9600 • Fax: 703-575-5400
Website: www.ascd.org • Email: member@ascd.org
Author guidelines: www.ascd.org/write

Richard Culatta, *Chief Executive Officer;* Anthony Rebora, *Chief Content Officer;* Genny Ostertag, *Managing Director, Book Acquisitions & Editing;* Susan Hills, *Senior Acquisitions Editor;* Mary Beth Nielsen, *Director, Book Editing;* Miriam Calderone, *Editor;* Thomas Lytle, *Creative Director;* Donald Ely, *Art Director;* Georgia Park, *Senior Graphic Designer;* Circle Graphics, *Typesetter;* Kelly Marshall, *Production Manager;* Shajuan Martin, *E-Publishing Specialist;* Kathryn Oliver, *Creative Project Manager*

All web links in this book are correct as of the publication date below but may have become inactive or otherwise modified since that time. If you notice a deactivated or changed link, please email books@ascd.org with the words "Link Update" in the subject line. In your message, please specify the web link, the book title, and the page number on which the link appears.

PAPERBACK ISBN: 978-1-4166-3259-7   ASCD product #123033   n01/24
PDF EBOOK ISBN: 978-1-4166-3260-3; see Books in Print for other formats.
Quantity discounts are available: email programteam@ascd.org or call 800-933-2723, ext. 5773, or 703-575-5773. For desk copies, go to www.ascd.org/deskcopy.

Library of Congress Cataloging-in-Publication Data

Names: Sackstein, Starr, author.
Title: Student-led assessment : promoting agency and achievement through portfolios and conferences / Starr Sackstein.
Description: Arlington, VA : ASCD, [2024] | Includes bibliographical references and index.
Identifiers: LCCN 2023037730 (print) | LCCN 2023037731 (ebook) | ISBN 9781416632597 (paperback) | ISBN 9781416632603 (pdf)
Subjects: LCSH: Educational evaluation. | Student-led parent conferences. | Portfolios in education.
Classification: LCC LB2822.75 .S225 2024 (print) | LCC LB2822.75 (ebook) DDC 379.1/58—dc23/eng/20231017

LC record available at https://lccn.loc.gov/2023037730
LC ebook record available at https://lccn.loc.gov/2023037731

33 32 31 30 29 28 27 26 25 24   1 2 3 4 5 6 7 8 9 10 11 12

*Learning is an intensely personal experience,
and as we progress through our journeys, the command
to "know thyself" rings true in so many ways.*

*This book is dedicated to the many students who learn
to use their voices to advocate for change and
to the teachers bold enough to amplify their voices.*

Expertise is meant to be stretched and shared.

Student-Led Assessment

Promoting Agency and Achievement Through Portfolios and Conferences

Introduction

"Ms. Sackstein, I'm struggling to understand why I keep getting feedback about cohesion in my writing when I feel I'm using the strategies we learned to make it happen. When I ask my peers for support, they have difficulty giving me concrete ideas on improving the flow. Can you help me get unstuck?"

"Of course I can. Show me the spot where you are not cohesive in your writing, and let's talk about what it means to find a flow."

My student eagerly reshared her paper with me through Google Docs, highlighting a part of her text that was very choppy. She had excellent ideas but needed support with transitions to ensure a smooth flow of the sentences. After we validated her conclusion that the paragraph read a bit staccato, we discussed what it means to demonstrate cohesion and how transition words and phrases can be a part of the solution. We also talked about sentence variety, a skill few writers naturally understand. After our short conversation in class, she eagerly returned to her table and began revising transitional phrases and varying her sentence structure for readability and cohesion.

Conversations like this were a central part of the experience in my classes. Students spent a lot of time learning about themselves as learners and the content and skills they needed to be proficient in when communicating in writing. And since student voice is vital to understanding what students know and can do, creating authentic opportunities for them to express their challenges and successes is how we developed an authentic learning culture in our shared space.

My understanding of and comfort with being a true educator have shifted in various ways as I've demonstrated many of the tenets I ask my students to explore. When I was testing the structures that became the basis for my book *Hacking Assessment: 10 Ways to Go Gradeless in a Traditional Grades School* (Sackstein, 2015a), a couple of things became evident rather quickly. I wasn't as clear about my expectations and teaching as I thought I was, and though my students wanted to excel, they sometimes lacked the knowledge or skills to do so. No one ever questioned my commitment to my students or the relationships I developed, but as I reflected more deeply on my practice, I realized I could do better.

And so, I decided to make several fundamental changes.

I stopped grading everything students submitted, and then I eradicated grades during the learning period. Reflection practices became critical to our conversations about learning, and portfolios were the name of the game for tracking student progress. As I provided students with the vocabulary to be a part of the learning process with me, many eagerly took the baton and ran with it. However, in making these significant shifts, a conundrum surfaced. In New York City public schools, grades are required for report cards, and my efforts to change that for my students were an uphill battle of the Greek tragedy variety. I needed to find a way to communicate learning that didn't undo all the practices we were using in class. How could I give students the agency to partner in this process and still accurately share how they were progressing?

The answer was student-led assessment conferences.

Informal conferences were already on full display in my class all the time. Whether it was small-group instruction based on specific goals that groups had set or one-on-one conversations like the one at the start of this chapter, students were using our shared vocabulary about their growth in their reflections and conversation, so why not include them in this final process, too?

As these changes were underway in my classroom, I was also volunteering on the school's portfolio committee, where three colleagues and I did a ton of research, spoke with experts, and tried to distill that learning into a handbook for the whole school to use. With my deepening understanding of best practices around portfolio assessment and profound commitment to metacognition, I was uniquely poised to create a system in my learning space where students could be empowered to demonstrate their learning and discuss their level of mastery regularly. These conversations became the basis for students' grades.

Of course, it wasn't all sunshine and daisies immediately. Many students just wanted me to tell them their grades; others vehemently resisted a grade, convinced by my own resistance to grading that it wasn't necessary. Together, we came to understand that regardless of whether grades were a necessary evil, assessment conferences were an integral part of how students demonstrated learning. Students saw them as a chance to talk about growth, set goals, and dig deeper if particular learning experiences didn't provide ample opportunity to show what they knew.

If you're interested in how we got to this point, feel free to read one of my earlier books, such as the aforementioned *Hacking Assessment* or *Assessing with Respect: Everyday Practices That Meet Students' Social and Emotional Needs* (Sackstein, 2021). This book centers on the processes and structures needed to develop a culture where student-led conferences become a vehicle for students to discuss their goals and learning and how teachers can include them in more decision making.

The book is organized in three parts to set the stage for building structures in your class alone or on a broader school- or districtwide scale:

- Part 1 is all about building systems that promote learner agency. The chapters in this section explore how to create a learning culture and clarity for learning as well as the formative assessment process, with a focus on reflection and building portfolio structures.
- Part 2 discusses how to build and adapt conferring protocols for the classroom.
- Part 3 explores the implementation of student-led assessment conferences using a gradual release of control approach.

Each chapter ends with reflection questions and activities to get you thinking about what these strategies could look like in your class. In addition, you will read special Perspective sections and testimonials from a variety of educators who have engaged in this work and who see the value it brings to their students. I encourage you to consider these case studies and other specific examples both in their specific contexts and in your own. This may require you to consider such factors as your students' ages and the content you teach. Obviously, good teaching strategies can work in a variety of settings and with a variety of age groups, so if there isn't an example that explicitly speaks to your context, try to imagine how the strategy would work for your students.

Over the years, many folks have asked me about this process and have marveled at the student videos I've shared that show my students' growth over the course of one year. Although this is challenging work, my only regret is that I didn't start doing it sooner. When I think about how it could have significantly improved the learning experiences of the many kids I've worked with, I feel sad that I wasn't "there" yet when I met them.

The strategies in this book support equitable assessment and grading practices. As we elevate each child's voice in class, we provide more opportunities to close the gap between *what we think* about their knowledge and skills and *what they know*. Believe it or not, no matter how well we have designed an assessment, our ability to see the depth of any child's growth honestly is incomplete without their ability to share it with us in a way that works for them.

The national narrative around learning loss created by the COVID-19 pandemic begs us to confront why we keep doing what we have always done long after realizing it doesn't work. The pandemic starkly highlighted existing inequities between different socioeconomic groups. When we take a personalized approach to righting such challenges, we are better equipped to serve more students where they are and change the narrative from one of loss to one of empowerment.

Thank you for taking the opportunity to explore the ways of knowing your students presented in this book. Trust the process, and you will learn more about your kids than you ever thought possible.

Part 1

Building Structures to Promote Learner Agency

For real change to take hold in any learning environment, we must nurture a culture that provides ample opportunity for student agency. I'm not talking about the nominal kind of agency where we give false choices or claim that kids have a say, but a rich culture where we truly teach them to use their voices in productive ways to advance our shared learning culture.

In this section, we will explore the building blocks of teaching students to talk about their learning in cohesive and detailed ways—not just to communicate what they have learned, but also to advocate for themselves if they need help. We will also explore how students can use the metacognitive process to apply the skills they learn in new contexts.

As you read this section, consider jotting down notes about

- What currently aligns with what you are doing,
- What you'd like to be doing,
- Barriers to success that you face, and
- Possible solutions to try right away.

You know your context and students best, so be sure to adapt what you are reading to the specifics of your community so that you can use the practices effectively in your learning spaces.

1

Building a Learner Agency–Enhanced Environment

Perhaps it feels trite at this point to talk about student-centered learning spaces, as this idea has saturated educational theory and philosophy for at least a decade now. What baffles me is that despite this push to put students in charge of their learning, many more traditional practices still permeate classrooms throughout the country.

As a consultant and chief operating officer of an EdTech company that specifically works with school leaders, teacher teams, and students to shift grading and assessment practices, I'm uniquely positioned to have seen firsthand how little practices have changed in some areas.

Additionally, as a parent, I've sadly witnessed my child's dwindling interest in his learning as he approaches high school graduation. At the heart of his disinterest is a lack of connection to the people who teach him and a style of teaching that does little to support his independent learning style. Why haven't his teachers made more of an effort to get to know him? During the COVID-19 pandemic, he thrived as a virtual student for an entire year. At the same time, he grew increasingly isolated from his school community. If we are going to create spaces where students thrive, this kind of isolation simply can't happen.

If you are a leader, ask yourself the hard questions about your classroom or school as you read this book: Does everyone in your space feel they belong? Do you honor the dignity and needs of all learners? If you answer yes, I suspect you build robust relationships that allow for multidirectional dialogue. You are most likely also open to genuine feedback and making any necessary adjustments to your practice.

Building Relationships Is Central to Learner Agency Environments

At the heart of our students' successes is our knowledge of them as human beings and learners. The better we know them, the better we can help them. It simply can't be overstated how meaningful building relationships in your classroom is—not just between you and the students, but among the students themselves. Our students won't take the kinds of risks we need them to take in the learning process if we don't provide them with ample opportunities to build trusting relationships with their peers.

As you start the school year, plan for time to get to know your learners and for them to know each other. Whatever your go-to relationship-building activity is—an interest survey, say, or a "find someone who" activity—make sure you participate. Kids need to know you as a learner and not just as their teacher. I'm not suggesting you share inappropriate personal details in the classroom, but I recommend you share your interests, strengths, and challenges so that students understand you are more like them than they realize. You, too, once sat where they sit, and perhaps you still do now if you're in a graduate program. Being a learner is vulnerable work, so never fail to acknowledge your understanding and gratitude for students' willingness to share whatever they do and to have patience with those who may be more reticent. Trust is earned, and nowhere is this more evident than in the learning process.

Establishing a Culture of Learning for All Learners

So, what does a culture of learning look like? Think about young children and the depth of curiosity they bring to their environment. If they aren't exploring new spaces, they may ask a barrage of rapid-fire questions that can catch us off guard if we're unprepared. Rather than be annoyed by these questions, be glad that students are eager to better understand the world they live in.

As educators, we are uniquely positioned to create spaces that invite curiosity and nurture it. Whether you are a kindergarten teacher exposing students to new ideas every day or a high school English teacher hoping to spark a love of challenging literature, how you introduce students to these ideas matters. You must make intentional choices and transparently share why you've made them until students can actively partake in the process with you.

Every learner is different, yet too many classrooms treat learners identically, which can kill opportunity. Some students are so accustomed to not being seen that we have to fight to ensure that they are. Just because a student isn't sharing their unique light doesn't mean it doesn't exist; it just means no one has ever taken the time to let it shine.

As we enter into relationships with the new kids in our spaces, we must behave like detectives or archaeologists, eager to uncover the greatest assets our students have to offer. Approach every student with real interest and warmth, model what vulnerability looks like, and show that you, too, are learning as you invite your seemingly most disengaged kids to contribute.

Creating a culture where all students are seen takes time, but the results will always be worth it. Here are a few strategies to consider that can ensure your efforts succeed:

- **Stand at the door and welcome every single child.** When you do this, try to notice the small stuff, like a new haircut or piercing, and pay each student a genuine compliment. If a student is returning to class after an absence, welcome them back with enthusiasm and remind them of the contribution they make in class (e.g., "Great to see you today! Class isn't the same without you.").
- **Always assume positive intent.** Even if a student has a misstep, assume the best intentions. You can express your concerns in a way that doesn't sound like an accusation right out of the gate.
- **Transparently correct your own mistakes.** If you want to create an environment that normalizes mistakes and failure, start with yourself. When you make a mistake, promptly admit your error, apologize if appropriate, and seek to rectify it with the group publicly. Early in my career, I was afraid to be wrong in front of kids, deeply concerned that it would ruin my credibility. But the longer I was in the classroom, the more I came to understand that being open about everything I didn't know and the process I went through to learn about things was far more palatable for my students than me always being right.
- **Create and post anchor charts for important ideas and leave them up.** Students learn at different rates, so we want to give them multiple opportunities

to engage with important ideas at different times. Anchor charts help with the transfer of learning and aid students in connecting and remembering ideas more deeply. They also allow students to save face if they aren't completely dialed in at a given moment.

- **Be mindful of the energy your space creates.** Although we want lots of text-rich spaces, we need to know our kids. Students with sensory challenges can be overwhelmed by a lot of stimuli on the walls, so be sure you know how much is too much. Don't be afraid to ask students privately if the space accommodates their needs.

Positive Expectations and Equitable Opportunities

Promoting high classroom expectations in a positive way is essential. It starts with remembering that "all kids *can*." Nothing is more distressing than hearing a frustrated educator say, "That's awesome, but my kids can't do that." The word *can't* comes up a lot in spaces where folks are focusing too heavily on what isn't going right. In those moments, I challenge you to see the bigger picture. Instead of saying a student can't do something, try to figure out the root causes and proceed with caution. What barrier is the student facing, and how can you and they work together to overcome it? We want all learners in our spaces to believe that success is possible, especially if they don't feel this way in other spaces. It's also important to recognize that knowing where students come from and what they value can help us to honor them in ways that help them see themselves as successful learners.

Developing a culture of learning is all about honoring the dignity of students and exploring who they are and where they come from to better serve them. It is also essential that we create the conditions for students to see one another as complete individuals and learn as much as they can about their unique backgrounds. The more we bring all of ourselves into the classroom every day and learn about our differences, the more we can acknowledge our similarities and bridge potential misunderstandings.

Part of building strong relationships is providing equitable opportunities for all kids. Remember that fair isn't always equal, as Rick Wormeli puts it in his 2006 book of the same name. Every child should have access to what they need to experience success. This is why co-constructing success criteria and learning experiences with students is key to fostering their confidence in new learning. When students have a hand in creating how they will demonstrate new learning, they gain clarity on how to be successful.

Too often, we assume kids know what to do because we give them directions, but that isn't always the case. To be honest, in my career, I was often a lot less clear than I thought I was, and that was often evidenced in students' grades. This wasn't the kids' issue; it was a "me" issue. These kinds of situations are extremely frustrating, and there were times I took that frustration out on the kids, which wasn't cool at all. There's real shame involved in that aspect of it. But having had those experiences allowed me to reflect and adjust. The first thing I decided to do was complete the assignments or projects I was assigning to students. Doing so enabled me to anticipate where students might struggle and where giving them a choice in their learning would be appropriate. Did I want them to choose which product to create? To have a say in how they would complete it? Ultimately, completing the assignments allowed me to see where and how the choice aspect would best fit. I was better able to talk to students about the assignments, and we could collaborate to ensure that they

1. Knew the purpose of the assignment and what the learning outcomes were.
2. Understood how this learning opportunity could enhance their lives outside the classroom.
3. Engaged with a deep understanding of what success looks like before starting— that is, that they knew the destination before they started the journey.
4. Had access to help, whether from me or from other experts, along the way. No rules say you can't ask for help while you're learning. Encouraging and supporting students to ask for help as soon as they realize they are stuck can help them overcome struggles before they lead to a shut-down level of frustration.
5. Had opportunities to offer suggestions or ideas for how they can accomplish the learning if it differs from the expected outcome. We always want to ensure that students understand there isn't only one right way to approach or complete a task; no one way is better than another so long as it gets the job done.

Portfolios to Promote a Positive Learning Journey

Progress isn't always easy to see. As teachers, we are dialed into it because we have been trained by time to recognize benchmark reminders of small steps taken to reach a greater goal. However, those small steps are not always visible to the learners who are taking them. Portfolios are essentially snapshots of learning kept in one place to make learning growth tangible. Think about when children are little and hit a growth spurt. Portfolios are like the little ticks on the wall we make to demonstrate growth, and even the most reluctant learners are usually excited to see that they're making progress.

There is nothing more gratifying than starting a challenging task or journey and seeing it through to its fruition, knowing that dedication and perspiration can will a goal into reality. In my own life, I've felt this gratification after finishing my first year of teaching, completing a degree, writing a book, achieving National Board Certification, and being recognized by the Dow Jones News Fund as a Special Recognition Adviser. This last recognition was for work that took nearly a decade to complete. Many times over those years, I felt like I was moving backward (and probably was). Still, I was able to forge ahead, tracking my learning over time and finally having the courage to submit a portfolio of growth at the end.

More than collections, portfolios highlight the infinitesimal movement forward that isn't always easy for us to see. They can empower students to set and track goals and promote continuous growth at a pace unique to every child. When we use portfolios, students must understand why we're doing so and how they will allow them to see their progress more clearly. Portfolios will also help them remember struggles that may slip away as they become more adept in the journey. Additionally, portfolios can help to de-emphasize the importance of arbitrary labels like grades on learning by demonstrating tangible movement forward. When we focus too heavily on markers like grades, we cheapen successes and promote the idea that someone else's validation is more important than our learning.

Creating Safe Spaces to Learn

When I worked as a classroom teacher and curriculum leader, promoting learning cultures was at the center of my working experiences. Even when I wasn't particularly practiced with my pedagogy, developing lasting relationships with students was a hallmark of our shared spaces. Whether working with diverse high school students or awkward middle school learners, seeing them and adapting to their needs made our shared spaces warm and welcoming.

One year early in my assessment and grading adventure, I had a rather uncomfortable confrontation with a student in my newspaper class. She made a comment that felt out of turn and even slightly personal. In response, I raised my voice much louder than was usual for me; I jarred even myself, and my embarrassment must have been palpable. I'm sure my face reddened, given the warmth I felt emanating from my neck. The bell was about to ring, and I could tell I had hurt the student's feelings— something I prided myself on *not* doing. At the sound of the bell, a stampede of outgoing and incoming students commenced, and I couldn't catch up with the young woman immediately. The more I dwelled on the situation, the worse I felt.

A few periods later, I found her walking in the hallway. On the verge of tears, I apologized profusely for reacting as I had. Even if what she'd said was off base, it was out of line for me to publicly reprimand her, and I was just sick about it. To further correct the misstep, I publicly apologized to her and the rest of the class the next day, as my behavior was the direct opposite of what I always espoused. We didn't spend all period harping on it, but once I'd had the chance to formally make amends and share what I had learned from the experience, it felt like the life came back into the room.

Learning is messy, and we *will* all make mistakes. How we react to these mistakes and seek to repair any harm they cause will make a lasting impression on the learning environments we create. To truly build long-standing valuable relationships where learning will thrive, we must live the tenets we espouse and acknowledge our humanness as a part of that process. All learners in the environment must feel like they are allowed to be wrong and that there is always a way back to the path. We have to model that generously. In this way, we genuinely teach by doing and learning as a shared experience with the other folks in our spaces.

It goes without saying that I also made many mistakes and was often harshly judged by my teachers when I first became a leader. Rather than allow those experiences to define how we functioned as a team, I reflected on my mistakes and shared the outcome of those reflections. More important, I tried not to make the same mistake more than once. I wanted folks to feel safe trying new things knowing they would always have my support, but I also needed them to know that their first attempts at new pedagogical practices weren't necessarily going to be easy or smooth.

Chapter Conclusions and Reflections

Elevating learners in our environments to truly own their learning is the first step to helping them connect with themselves in this process. When we create spaces that acknowledge differences and highlight how our differences strengthen us, each person can find a space to shine and matter to the collective whole. It is then that we can truly develop a collective efficacy in the group for the betterment of all.

Now that you've read this chapter, take some time to think about your current situation. What evidence do you have that you've developed a learner-centered space and a broader learning community? What are your strengths, and how do you know? Can you systematize and share these strengths with colleagues? What gaps do you need to dive more deeply into? What do you fear about making significant changes to your approach?

Developing a positive learning atmosphere in our schools means being defiant in the face of our discomfort or fear and taking the necessary risks to elevate learning above all else. Doing these things will pave the way for all the challenging and exciting things we are about to explore.

2

Promoting Clarity to Deepen Student Understanding

Have you ever asked students to complete a task or a project, providing them with what you think are clear and explicit directions, only to get a dozen different kinds of projects—and a feeling in your gut that perhaps it's all your fault? Worse yet, have you ever blamed any confusion on the students for not following your directions properly? Early in my career, before I started actually completing my own assignments before asking students to do so, I often got angry when students just didn't do what I asked them to do. What I soon learned is that clarity isn't as easy as it sounds. Sometimes we don't communicate what we expect to communicate, even when we think we're being crystal clear.

Teacher clarity is essential to achieving student clarity, which John Hattie suggests has a .75 effect size, or almost two years' worth of learning in one year. In this chapter, we explore ways to help gain and promote clarity in the classroom throughout the learning process.

Selecting Priority Standards for Content and Skills

The first time an educator reviews the Common Core or any other set of standards, they are bound to be confused or overwhelmed. There is so much to cover, and so much of what is there is vaguely written. School teams must consider graduation requirements and backward-plan vertically to deduce what standards are most relevant to them. It is only once core knowledge and skills are identified that teachers can move on to focusing on standards. Larry Ainsworth (2013) suggests organizing knowledge and skills into three categories as a means to decide what is really necessary and what is just an extra. The categories are as follows:

1. **Endurance:** Knowledge and skills of value beyond a single assessment date
2. **Leverage:** Knowledge and skills of value in multiple disciplines
3. **Readiness:** Knowledge and skills necessary for success in the next grade level or the next level of instruction

You can learn more about how you and your team can select priority or essential standards in Larry Ainsworth's (2013) book *Prioritizing the Common Core.* Additional resources to support prioritizing standards can be found here (as well as in the References and Resources list in the back of this book):

- "Facilitation Guide to Prioritizing Standards," by the Michigan Assessment Consortium: www.michiganassessmentconsortium.org/wp-content/uploads /Facilitation-Guide-Prioritizing-Standards.pdf
- "Identifying Essential Standards," by Solution Tree: www.allthingsplc.info /files/uploads/identifying-essential-standards-presentation.pdf
- "Priority Standards Deep Dive: What You Should Know," by Edmentum: https:// blog.edmentum.com/priority-standards-deep-dive-what-you-should-know

Unpacking Learning Standards or Competencies

Once you've selected your priority standards, the next step is to ensure you understand your curriculum's expectations. Whether you are backward planning from graduation requirements or state expectations, you must know the agreed-upon overarching competencies, learning standards, and content knowledge that students are expected to demonstrate by the end of the year.

Regardless of how well you know your content, it is always a good idea to practice unpacking standards with your teacher team so that everyone has a shared understanding of keywords and concepts and an agreed-upon idea of what proficiency looks like. There are various ways to unpack standards, but most center on breaking them down into verbs and nouns and figuring out the depth of knowledge required to meet them in different contexts. Figure 2.1 shows an example of the format the Core Collaborative counsels teacher teams to use for unpacking standards. (A blank template of this form can be found in Appendix A on page 150.)

Figure 2.1.　Sample Completed Template for Unpacking Standards

Focus Standard Clusters

Focus Standards

- W.2.1 Write opinion pieces in which they introduce the topic or book they are writing about, state an opinion, supply reasons that support the opinion, use linking words (e.g., *because*, *and*, *also*) to connect opinion and reasons, and provide a concluding statement or section.
- W.2.5 With guidance and support from adults and peers, focus on a topic and strengthen writing as needed by revising and editing.
- RI.2.8 Describe how reasons support specific points the author makes in a text.

Supporting Standards

- W.2.6 With guidance and support from adults, use a variety of digital tools to produce and publish writing, including in collaboration with peers.
- L.2.2 Demonstrate command of the conventions of standard English capitalization, punctuation, and spelling when writing.
- L.2.3 Use knowledge of language and its conventions when writing, speaking, reading, or listening.

Research the Standards

- Reading comprehension and writing are cyclical. Students have to practice them again and again and understand how skills and concepts are connected and build on one another. Part of the learning process is being clear about which scaffolds support learning at each level.
- Keys for second revision:
  — Focuses on a topic
  — Revises
  — Edits
- Many students need support with sentences, paragraphs, and other organization.
- Determining "reasons that support the opinion" is difficult for many students and requires being able to draw connections between information and determine importance.
- Some learners think through their ideas better orally and may need support in productive writing.
- Students may need to learn it's OK for people to disagree with them! "Your job is to support your thinking and to listen or read carefully to understand the reasons, evidence, and opinions of others. It's not to agree with the teacher or your friends."
- This standard lends itself to projects that have an impact on the learner's community.
- Understanding how authors support points with reasons strengthens students' writing and comprehension of what they read.

(continued)

Figure 2.1. Sample Completed Template for Unpacking Standards (Continued)

Concepts to Unpack

- Reasons and evidence
- Types of reasoning—statistics/facts, emotional appeal, authority of author(s) or source(s)
- Justifications
- Differentiating between facts and opinions
- Revision and editing
- Paragraph- and grouping-related ideas
- Argument
- Debate

Leverage Vertical Learning Progressions

Prerequisite Knowledge and Skills	Accelerated Knowledge and Skills
<ul><li>Simply introduce the topic or name the book students are writing about.</li><li>Students may only supply one reason for their opinion.</li><li>Students need to be able to provide some sense of closure.</li><li>Students receive more guidance and support from adults to plan, compose, and revise their work.</li><li>Students begin to respond to questions and suggestions from peers, as well as providing their own reflection, to add details to strengthen writing as needed.</li><li>Students need to be able to simplify and identify the reasons an author gives to support points in a text.</li></ul>	<ul><li>More opinions and arguments will focus on simple analysis of texts.</li><li>Students support a point of view with reasons.</li><li>Students create an organizational structure that connects multiple reasons.</li><li>Students use more specific linking words and phrases to connect reasons to opinions.</li><li>Students support a point of view with reasons.</li><li>Planning and revision become more of a focus in the writing process.</li><li>Expectations for editing are increased (see L.3.1–3).</li><li>Students describe the logical connection between sentences and paragraphs in a text (e.g., comparison, cause/effect, first/second/third in a sequence), developing their understanding of text structure and analyzing the relationship between support and evidence and the author's claim.</li></ul>

Learning Intentions	
Essential Question/Goal(s)	**Big Ideas**
• What makes a good argument? How would you win an argument with someone in your family? • How does an author make sure their audience understands their opinion? • How can we use drafting, feedback, and revision in other areas of our learning?	• Writers connect reasons and evidence to support opinions in writing that are appropriate to the audience and purpose. If we want someone to take our opinion or argument seriously, we need good facts to back up what we are saying. • The writing process involves planning, drafting, editing, and revising a piece for clarity and cohesiveness. Writing is not a one-step process. Writers revisit the paper and ideas many times before they publish to improve flow and descriptions and check for mechanical errors. This is the same process for learning anything. You start with a goal, try it, and revise it and then move on. • Writing is only finished when you decide it's ready for your audience. To publish a piece, we expect to go back and revise many times!

The Learning Process		
Success Criteria/Learning Targets		
Surface Criteria	**Deep Criteria**	**Transfer Criteria**
• Define and describe important concepts and parts of opinion papers, including the following: — Opinion — Topic	• Independently write an opinion piece that includes an introduction, reasons with supporting details, and conclusion.	**Near Transfer** • Explain how others are using arguments/opinions to persuade me (e.g., through advertising).

(continued)

Figure 2.1. Sample Completed Template for Unpacking Standards (Continued)

Surface Criteria	Deep Criteria	Transfer Criteria
— Introduction — Conclusion or concluding statement — Linking words • Use a variety of linking words (e.g., *because*, *and*, *so*) to connect ideas. • List and define the phases of the writing process. • List and recognize the conventions of writing (see L.2). • Describe the editing process. • State my opinions on a topic. • Use digital tools to create and improve my writing.	• Recognize and explain when facts are used as opinions. • Recognize and explain when opinions are used as facts. • Choose and justify reasons that support my opinion. • Evaluate the quality of reasons ("Does this reason support the opinion/argument?"). • Choose appropriate linking words that connect my opinion and reasons. • Explain the difference between revising and editing. • Edit a little bit at a time throughout the writing process. • Decide how to revise to make the writing clear, informative, descriptive, and convincing. • Determine when and how to edit for conventions (see L.2, L.3). • Determine which digital tools to use to create or improve my writing. • Analyze the suggestions given by peers and decide which feedback to apply.	• Pull from exemplars and mentor texts to revise my own writing. • Edit a writing piece in any subject area using correcting conventions. • Decide when it is time to revise or edit a piece. • Provide feedback that improves my peers' writing. **Far Transfer** • Revise *any* writing piece in any genre so the topic is clear, well-developed, and easy to understand. • Justify and evaluate claims in other content areas (e.g., I agree with how X solved the problem because . . . ; I don't think X was right because . . .). • Develop and share an opinion, supported by reasons, about a topic that impacts you or your classmates.

Surface Learner Strategies	Deep Learner Strategies	Transfer Learner Strategies
• Jigsaw method • Integrating prior knowledge • Summarization • Mnemonics • Direct instruction • Record keeping • Note taking • Asking "Who?" "What?" and "How?"	• Organizing and transforming notes • Identifying underlying similarities and differences • Classroom discussion • Reciprocal teaching • Concept mapping • Metacognitive strategy instruction • Self-questioning • Teacher questioning • Inquiry-based teaching • Simulations • Asking "How?" • Asking "Why?"	• Transforming conceptual knowledge • Organizing conceptual knowledge • Formal discussions • Problem-solving teaching • Reading and synthesizing across documents • Peer tutoring • Asking "Should?" "Where?" "When?" and "To what extent?"
Brainstorm Formative Tasks		
Surface Tasks for New Learning	Impact Team Deep Tasks	Impact Team Transfer Tasks

• Guided analysis of exemplars
  — Labeling and defining parts of an opinion piece
  — Highlighting/ annotating criteria
• Annotating opinion writing orally and in writing based on structure and relationships
• Completing a simple graphic organizer to plan
	• Comparing examples and nonexamples
	• Writing an opinion paragraph that includes a reason and evidence to support it
	• Writing opinion papers
	• Revising nonexamples or your own papers based on the success criteria (focusing on one or two criteria at a time)
		Near Transfer
		
		• Revising and editing your own work
		• Changing the form of the writing (e.g., essay to speech, graphic organizer/ notes to debate)
		• Planning for and engaging in a debate based on the writing project
		• Providing feedback that improves a peer's writing

(continued)

Figure 2.1. Sample Completed Template for Unpacking Standards (Continued)

Surface Tasks for New Learning	Impact Team Deep Tasks	Impact Team Transfer Tasks
• Describing types of reasons • Taking quizzes and proving learning for concepts	• Justifying decisions about your writing during a writing conference • Annotating your own or a peer's writing using the success criteria • Revising to include a variety of quality reasons that are supported by reliable sources and connected to the opinion	**Far Transfer** • Writing opinion papers across subject areas • Writing an informational piece that supports your opinion or claim • Writing a narrative that uses characters' experiences to support your opinion or claim • Planning a project to apply your new skills of supporting opinions with reasons (e.g., by taking on an issue in school or the community that impacts the class and co-creating a plan to influence decision-makers)

Self-Regulation of Core Habits of Learning

Academic Capacity	Emotional Capacity	Social Capacity
☐ Perseverance ☑ Questioning and problem posing ☑ Quality communication ☐ Thinking interdependently ☑ Metacognition ☐ Thinking flexibly ☐ Other	☐ Self-awareness ☑ Empathy ☑ Openness and vulnerability ☐ Patience ☐ Humility ☐ Compassion ☐ Other	☑ Listening to understand ☐ Thinking interdependently ☐ Openness and vulnerability ☑ Patience ☑ Precise communication ☐ Other

Resources and Strategies to Teach Standards	
Resources	**Page**
Citation:	

In Figure 2.1, notice the focus-standard clusters, where teams select the standard or standards they wish to unpack. This robust format has the team not only separate verbs and nouns as skills and concepts, but also look at whole clusters of standards and supporting practices. The team researches the standard and breaks it down according to conceptual understanding, procedural fluency, and application. Then, the team examines learning progressions by reviewing standards for the preceding and succeeding grade levels, identifying both prerequisite and accelerated knowledge and skills. Next, the team considers learning intentions via essential questions and big ideas, which cue them to consider the learning process, deepen their understanding of the particular focus-standard cluster, and dive more deeply into how it will look in practice. The team explores the cluster's surface-, deep-, and transfer-level learning and considers formative activities to use with students. At the bottom of the form, the team includes additional resources.

Once a team unpacks a single standard or cluster of standards, a school can develop a library of unpacked standards that new teams can explore and revise over time. This can offer grade-level teams and school communities both clarity and a shared opportunity to build efficacy. The more we use the same language and processes to dig deeply into planning, the better equipped students will be from year to year, regardless of their teacher.

Using Learning Targets Aligned with Standards

After taking the time to unpack priority standards, you must create student-friendly learning targets. Students need to understand what they are supposed to learn and how they can succeed in doing so. Think of learning targets as bite-size versions of any standards you are working on. A learning target makes a standard digestible and assessable in a smaller time frame.

Learning targets—aims, objectives, outcomes, and so on—are short, active statements that provide a clear lens through which to explore a small aspect of the curriculum on any given day (or over multiple days). Learning targets allow you to intentionally chunk standards into smaller bites to ensure all students are learning every aspect of a particular standard prior to any summative assessment. These targets should be displayed and shared with students so that they can understand expectations before the learning routine starts. Students should be able to look at a specific location in the room when they arrive to class and know what to expect for the day. But merely posting a learning target is simply not enough; you must also ensure the target's language and level of clarity are reflected throughout the lesson.

An emphasis on clarity promotes opportunities to build a shared vocabulary that helps students to discuss their learning and enriches their self-advocacy. Though the importance of shared vocabulary is often overlooked, it can prevent various challenges down the road.

Building Student-Facing Learning Progressions

Learning progressions allow teachers and students to see how a skill or concept builds in complexity over time. The Core Collaborative template for unpacking standards (see Appendix A, p. 150) offers a vocabulary for discussing learning progressions and gives students and teachers the ability to pinpoint exactly what a student knows and can do. Kids can point to their work and set goals for where they want to go next.

To create student-facing learning progressions, start by examining a crosswalk of a vertical progression of a standard and adjusting the language to be more kid-friendly. You want students to be able to read and understand the specifics of the progression so that they can use these documents for self- and peer assessments along the way.

Learning progressions give students the tools they need to understand the language of the standards and then use that understanding to promote a deeper understanding of what they know and what they need to know, building their efficacy as learners.

Figure 2.2 shows how high school Latin teacher Lance Piantaggini helps students with process standards.

Co-Constructing Success Criteria for Optimal Student Success

The next step to ensuring clarity is developing success criteria, mentioned earlier in this chapter. To achieve the optimal learning experience, students need to know what success looks like. You will need to provide your students with success criteria until using them becomes a part of the routine. Once students know what success criteria are and how to use them, you can begin to include students in the co-construction process, giving them more control. Unlike most rubrics, which let students know the learning target of a lesson, success criteria break that target down into smaller pieces for them to shoot for, as with a checklist.

I encourage you to move away from rubrics that assess learning according to a 4-point scale, as these essentially give students a roadmap to being less than proficient. If level 3 reflects proficiency, why tell students how to achieve at levels 1 and 2? In my experience, this essentially permits them to do subpar work. Instead, I recommend using a single-point rubric focused on success criteria for meeting the standard that leaves room for reflection and feedback, as shown in Figure 2.3.

The rubric in Figure 2.3 provides clear expectations with specific success criteria as well as language for providing themselves or a peer with feedback. If the student needs to improve in an area, constructive feedback with a strategy for improvement can be offered in the Grow column of the rubric, and validation for work done well can go in the Glow column.

Students must understand where success criteria are coming from and what they look like. Research (Dean et al., 2012) tells us that students need models to be successful, so we want to ensure we model the process of developing success criteria before they start on the assignment. Once students have had multiple opportunities to see success criteria and how they are created, we can invite them into the

Figure 2.2. Latin Learning Progressions

Process Standard

You receive a lot of comprehensible input (CI).
The process of Latin you understand (comprehensible) coming into your mind (input) is achieved by looking and listening and responding/showing/asking.

Looking: Awareness of what's happening in class (e.g., board, wall, book, laptop, etc.)
Listening: Awareness of what's being spoken in class, to you, and to others
Responding: Answering questions and reacting out loud
Showing: Reacting nonverbally in a way that shows understanding
Asking: Signaling and/or stopping when Latin isn't clear so you understand

Not Looking and Listening: Using phones, doing other classwork, having book open to the wrong page, being on other websites, distracting doodling, talking over someone, leaving the room, sleeping
Not Responding/Showing/Asking: Being confused, not understanding *all* the Latin

Growth Standard

Growing
Older texts seem easier to read and/or current ones *feel like* my reading level.

Growth: New texts feel like you can read them without hesitation, with the exception of new specific words that won't repeat as much in other texts (e.g., spooky vocab for the spooky book).
My Reading Level: Texts you can understand without having to look up words are below- or at-level. The fewer words you have to look up, and the fewer times you hesitate to understand, the easier the text.
Potential: At-level texts represent what is possible for approaching a challenge.

Not Growing: New texts feel harder and cause you to hesitate, even when there aren't many new specific words. New texts with words found in older texts and ones that repeat a lot during class (e.g., *vult, habet, sunt, putat, Quomodo*, etc.).
Not My Reading Level: Texts that you can't understand without a glossary and that make you hesitate while reading are above-level.
Not Potential: These texts are far away from being challenging, even though it's possible for you to read others at a higher level.

Source: Courtesy of Lance Piantaggini. Used with permission.

Figure 2.3. Single-Point Rubric Example

Grow	Criteria	Glow
	Claim is clear and takes a position that directly relates to the prompt.	
	Context is clear to situate the reader.	
	Organization is such that the reader knows what to expect as they continue through the rest of the paragraphs.	
	Mechanics don't inhibit understanding of the presented ideas.	

Source: Copyright 2023 The Core Collaborative. Used with permission.

process and amplify the agency they have in demonstrating how to create success criteria aligned with specific tasks and standards.

Co-constructing success criteria means looking at an assignment together with students and eliciting their ideas for developing the criteria. Students can be partners in both developing criteria and building the rubric. Once they are a part of this process, they are clear about expectations and will more readily find success because of it.

 PERSPECTIVE: Rosalia Tierno, Assistant Principal

When I first heard the phrase "co-constructing success criteria," I had taught for almost 20 years and was sitting in professional development with educators half my age. Honestly, my initial reaction to the proposed strategy was predictable for a veteran teacher being told to change their practice. Astonished by the idea of relinquishing control of the classroom to my students, I decided I would never use the technique. My stubborn outlook made the process of adopting the strategy difficult and time-consuming. After reviewing the PD materials and reading independently on the effectiveness of the practice, I had the stark realization that it had far less to do with the teacher's meticulously planned lessons and everything to do with student ownership of their learning and goal setting for all students.

Beginning to design lessons with this strategy was the most challenging step in my transition to using it. My effort was concentrated on crafting solid, standards-based learning intentions so all students understood their learning target for the day. Well-written learning intentions resulted in more effective tasks and formative assessments that helped students decipher the steps necessary to achieve the day's goal.

Allowing a margin of error for those first few lessons is vital. Cautiously approaching the lesson with full acknowledgment that it may flop and guiding students to the right answer is the only way to muddle through the process. But then one day, after reading the learning intention aloud and relying on the models from the previous days, a typically quiet young man raised his hand. "Don't we need to know what the definition of political parties is to identify the role they play in our government?" he asked.

It was a moment of inspiration that has lasted to this day.

Students understood they could dictate the knowledge they attained in a 44-minute class period, and genuinely accepted and internalized the learning. One student became two, then four, until the whole class was discussing our two or three bullets of success criteria daily. This process revealed what interested them, what they wanted to learn, what would help them understand the content, and what skills they felt they needed to master a standard and target.

I cannot remember what my classes were like before I made co-constructing success criteria part of my daily routine. My students do not know any other way. We co-construct the success criteria for the day, the unit, and the semester from the first lesson of the year. Immediately, students learn to set goals that will aid in their progression toward mastering the standards for their grade level. Soon the process becomes a habit. They can outline criteria for rubrics, projects, and performance tasks. The co-constructing informs the teacher how to amend or enhance the curriculum, the next day's lessons, and the various learning assessments throughout the course. The benefits of this practice change a teacher's outlook on their planning, classroom, and students.

Today, as an assistant principal, I hope that the teachers I lead understand my support and encouragement to attempt co-constructing success criteria with their students while also acknowledging the patience it may take to make them true believers.

Exemplars and Modeling

According to instructional designer Tana Esplin, exemplars are "key examples chosen to be typical of designated levels of quality of competence" (quoted in Sadler, 2005). They can consist of authentic student work from previous classes or teacher-constructed examples based on the teacher's experience with common mistakes students make. These exemplars can help students increase their understanding of particular skills, content, or knowledge and internalize established criteria or standards. As Sadler (2010) notes, the concrete nature of exemplars conveys a message in a way nothing else can. They can help students "see" what to expect from an assignment (Scoles et al., 2012).

You may be saying to yourself, "If I provide a model of what I expect, won't students merely copy what I present?" I have heard this argument before and thought about it myself at times. Early in my career, I provided exact replications of the outcomes I expected, only to receive imitations from students who called them their own. Eventually I learned that it's best to provide an example using different content from what's in the assignment or to model the assignment using an accessible topic with which everyone is familiar.

When sharing models, make sure to demonstrate different ways of approaching the assignment so students don't feel limited in their creativity. You want them to know what you are looking for without prescribing a single "right" way to go about it. Of course, there are exceptions; if you teach math or science and require students to present their learning in a particular way, provide examples with varying levels of complexity rather than alternative ways of approaching the problem.

Finding this balance takes time. I recommend that teacher teams collect student samples over the years to create a library of exemplars they can use.

Differentiated Feedback

All learning requires feedback, and success criteria allow you to differentiate that feedback. Once you know what the learning target is, use the language of the criteria to tell students specifically what they are doing well and how to improve in certain areas. A single-point rubric is one easy way to do this, but it isn't the only way. You can also provide feedback directly in class, in informal conferences, and on documents.

Feedback should come from the students as well as the teacher. You have many opportunities to bring students into this process before formally assessing their learning. Use the success criteria to promote better self- and peer assessment feedback throughout the learning process. No student should have to wait until they submit their work to learn about something they could have caught and fixed earlier.

PERSPECTIVE: Emma Chiappetta, Instructional Coach and Math Teacher (Part 1)

As a young math teacher, I thought that you either had a student-centered classroom or you didn't. Throughout my journey, I've realized that it's more of a sliding scale, and I discover new levels of the scale every year (see Figure 2.4).

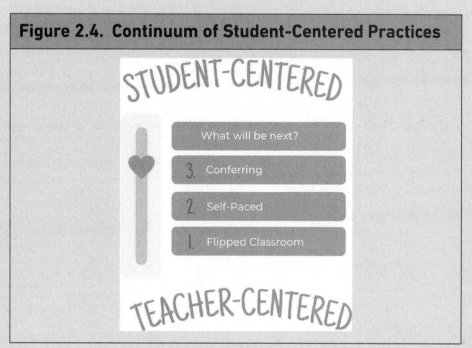

Figure 2.4. Continuum of Student-Centered Practices

Source: Courtesy of Emma Chiappetta. Used with permission.

Flipping my class was the first step I took. It allowed me to spend more time talking to students while they were working. These informal conversations gave me detailed insights into the mental schemas my students were building around the content. They allowed me to stop misconceptions in their tracks and provide personalized instruction. The next step was transitioning to a self-paced classroom that gave students control over the rate at which they learned. They practiced goal setting and reflected on when they felt ready to be assessed.

I was proud of my students and loved our classroom environment, but something was still missing. Some students, like Trevor, couldn't focus on written tasks, especially not on a unit test. Students like Jerry performed beautifully on their exams simply because they had learned to mimic the examples they had seen rather than because they truly understood the big ideas that tied the content together. Other students, like Sofia, had such low self-efficacy in math that they needed validation of their ideas at every step; they left questions unanswered on tests despite knowing the content.

The missing piece for these students was an assessment that would make their thinking visible, challenge them at the appropriate level, and respect their unique approach to learning: student conferences.

My first conferences were a bit clunky. They took too much time, I did too much talking, students didn't know what to say, and, honestly, I wasn't sure if they were fair. Over time, I've smoothed out the hiccups.

To make conferences effective, I am clear about my goals for them:

- Determine how well the student can contextualize the content in terms of a bigger picture.
- Assess the extent to which the student can execute the procedures required by the standard.
- Guide the student to self-reflect on their learning.
- Provide additional support or challenge as necessary.

These goals provide a sense of the conference structure. I begin with broad, big-picture questions, like these:

- What was this module all about?
- How does this module connect with what you learned in the previous module? How is it different?
- Can you explain, define, or give examples of the main concepts in this module?

Then, I ask more pointed questions requiring students to do some math. Usually, I have them create a problem to solve, which can be challenging. Next, I ask them to solve it on a whiteboard before me, describing the steps as they do so. I ask probing questions such as "How did you know to do that?" or "What if we changed the original problem to _____? How would your procedure change?"

At this stage, I may also provide feedback on mistakes or misconceptions students have demonstrated. Hearing them explain their logic helps me understand their thinking, honor where they are, and give them the most targeted support for improvement.

As they work through math problems, students with low math confidence may come to a place where they want to give up. In those cases, conferences allow me to write a similar but simpler problem next to the one they're working on. As they solve the simpler one, we note commonalities with the original problem, which almost always gives them direction for completing it. Students realize that they know much more than they think, and their self-efficacy grows.

For students who breeze through the material, conferences allow me to push them further by providing a more challenging problem or teasing out their knowledge of the module to come. Often, this piques their curiosity and develops into an energetic conversation.

At the end of the content-focused portion of the conference, I always ask, "Is there something that you put a lot of time into learning that we haven't talked about yet?" This allows students to show off, demonstrate the progress they've made since the last conference that I might not have noticed, or talk about additional learning they needed that I may not have been aware of.

Near the end of the conference is time for reflection. At the beginning of the year, I give students reflection prompts such as the following to get them thinking about what reflection means:

- What is a mistake you made that you won't make again?
- What was the most challenging part of this module, and what finally helped you understand it?
- What do you think you did well in this module?
- What is something you feel like you need to continue working on?

As the year goes on, I'll simply ask, "How was this module for you?" Students can then tell me about their learning journey. They often reflect throughout the conference, saying things like "This part was tough for me to understand at first, but . . ." or "I think I still need to work on this part a little bit."

We finish things off with self-assessment. By this point, we've had time to discuss all the pieces, and we end by determining where students fall on the learning progression. Each conference is geared toward only one content standard. Keeping students focused on only a few small learning targets increases efficiency and clarifies the learning targets to students. When they self-assess, they give themselves a score out of eight for their understanding of the content. They understand that eight means "I can do everything this module requires without help, and I understand the concepts." I usually agree with my students' assessments, and we talk about what they need to do to earn an eight. I might give them an alternate summative evaluation or more practice work to get them there. On the rare instance where we disagree, we talk about why, come to an agreement, and formulate a path forward.

Chapter Conclusions and Reflections

Clarity is an essential part of the learning process. If you want students to be able to speak to their learning in meaningful ways, you must first align your learning experiences and then provide ample opportunities for students to practice what they learn. Only in this way can they become the partners you want them to be and take full ownership of their learning.

Students can be invited into the learning process in various ways, and the sooner we include them, the more empowered they will become. As you reflect on the content of this chapter, consider the following questions:

- Do you have priority standards that you have unpacked with your colleagues for greater team efficacy?

- How are these priority standards taught, practiced, and assessed in your learning environment?
- How are your learning targets aligned to unpacked standards?
- Do you have up-to-date learning progressions for your priority standards that are student-facing?
- Can students speak to the standards and their progress on them? How do you know?
- What structures do you have in place to partner with students to ensure success?
- How do you model learning for students?

3

Using Formative Assessment to Promote Learner Voice and Self-Advocacy

When I took on the National Board Certification process, I was exposed to a level of professional reflection that I had not consciously or practically encountered before. Although I consider myself a naturally reflective person, I had not intentionally taken the time and energy to track my teaching until this experience. Since then, I have implemented rigorous academic student reflection in my classroom.

As I developed the system I would later coach others to use, I came to see the many benefits of student reflection, from balancing student voice and self-advocacy to differentiating for every single learner through personalized feedback. Reflection also gives students a routine way to track their growth and provide valuable feedback on their learning experiences, which in turn helped me to revise and craft better learning experiences and assessments. This iterative process was central to developing a learning synergy in the classroom that created a dynamic opportunity for growth.

In this chapter, we explore how the foundational understanding of the importance of clarity discussed in Chapter 2 promotes the formative assessment process, true student empowerment, and enhancement of curiosity in the classroom.

Helping Students to Understand the Formative Assessment Process

Before students explore and understand the formative assessment process, you all need to be on the same page about what it *is*. Rather than considering formative assessment as a single opportunity for learning, like an exit ticket, it is important to undergo a whole formative assessment cycle to ensure your students have ample practice and exposure to new ideas before they are summatively assessed on that same learning. Figure 3.1 shows some key differences between formative and summative assessment to help teachers and students see where ownership resides for each and the stakes involved in completion.

Once your students are clear about what formative assessment means, the next step is goal setting. Students should take the feedback they have received and create goals that are meaningful to them. Sometimes these goals will align with what you have planned for the year and sometimes won't; this is OK as long as all objectives are met by the end of the year.

Once they've set their goals, students need opportunities to practice using what they've learned, tracking progress on their goals as they do so. While they are working on this, you will have time to provide differentiated feedback either orally as you walk around the room, in writing on their papers when they submit learning, or on a recording if that works better for you. Students will then take your feedback and make the necessary revisions to deepen their understanding. These deliberate practice opportunities help students to identify areas where they are getting stronger but still facing challenges.

After students have had ample time to practice, get feedback, and make revisions, it's time for peer feedback. Provide students with a structure for developing concrete

Figure 3.1. Formative Assessment Versus Summative Assessment

Formative: Assessment FOR Learning	Summative: Assessment OF Learning
Purpose: To give feedback on learning and teaching	Purpose: To demonstrate achievement
Low stakes	High stakes
Students are responsible for their own learning.	Teachers are responsible for students' learning.
Examples: Written feedback to student, teacher-student dialogue, feedback to teacher to improve teaching	Examples: Graded end-of-semester exam, culminating project, GPA

goals. For example, depending on the ages of your students, you may want to use a TAG protocol (T = tell me something you like, A = ask a question, G = give some positive feedback to improve my work), a "glow and grow" protocol, or a ladder of feedback with sentence starters. Peer feedback isn't going to be great at first, so you'll need to provide your own feedback on the student feedback to help students improve it.

After students receive peer feedback, they revise their work until they are ready to self-assess using a rubric and success criteria. This should be the last round of revisions before the final product is submitted for summative review. It is at this point that students should be allowed to reflect on their learning. This metacognitive activity helps them solidify what they were working on, how they tackled challenges, what they would do differently, and so on. It will also help you to assess their learning. Take the opportunity to read a students' reflections before reviewing their work. You should be able to see how they self-assessed, what their process was, and what their goals are and provide tailored feedback based on their personalized experience.

At this point, students will review their growth to determine whether they have met the goals they set for themselves or if they should continue with the same goals because they aren't where they want to be yet. If they are ready to set new goals, now is an appropriate time to have that conversation with them.

At the end of the day, what you want to communicate with students always is that practice is what helps us grow as learners. They will have many opportunities to practice skills and use them in new ways with new learning, at which point the formative assessment process begins all over again.

Setting Goals Based on Feedback

In the beginning, it may make sense for a teacher to set goals for a student based on the data on their learning progress presented. However, it must be the goal of every teacher to eventually help students become adept at knowing themselves as learners and setting attainable goals so they can track their own progress daily.

At the start of the year, when you begin to build your relationships with students, you will learn their communication preferences and how best to share feedback with them. Rather than marking everything that needs correcting, you may want to focus on what's most important. For example, suppose you find a student has a large conceptual misunderstanding. In that case, getting them to rectify this misunderstanding is more important than addressing a careless computational error. What you decide to highlight in your feedback will help students choose their goals—and the more comfortable they get with the process, the less prompting they will need from you.

Once a student has set a goal, they should write it down and share it with the teacher and at least one peer. The sheer act of writing down goals is powerful; one research study (Schippers et al., 2020) even found it was a significant factor in increasing students' academic performance. It's not enough just to say we want to accomplish something; we must formally present our goals in writing. You can and should model this process for students, too. Teach them to track their goals with a measurable action plan that can be broken down into concrete steps. Remember as well that goals should be as specific as possible. (See Appendix C on page 156 for a sample student goal tracker.) As you provide each student with feedback, make sure your comments are specific to their action plan and let them know whether they're on track to meet their goals.

Student-created goals provide you with a framework for generating a personalized learning plan for each student. When you know what they are working toward, you can provide strategic feedback asking them to complete activities that align with their goals. It can be especially helpful to group students by their goals in classroom learning centers and provide them with personalized learning opportunities; Karen Terwilliger and I discuss this in depth in our 2021 book *Hacking Learning Centers in Grades 6–12*.

Teaching Reflection as a Part of the Process

Reflection is the act of intentionally considering our learning to share our understandings, explore challenges, and track our progress over time. Reflection is metacognitive—that is, it involves thinking about thinking. It's an opportunity for students to consider their process and look deeply into how they approached a task and whether they succeeded.

Reflection is often confused with self-assessment, which is more evaluative in nature. Figure 3.2 provides some examples of how the two practices differ. That being said, self-assessment will likely be a part of reflection—often the part that students gravitate toward. You must explicitly teach students to reflect *academically*—that is, to consider what they have learned with regard to specific skills and content (competences or standards)—or else you're liable to receive rants about what students liked or didn't like, which is not what you are looking for.

Some students require no more than a prompt to get started with reflection, while others need more extensive scaffolding. At a minimum, explain and provide an example of what reflection can be and why it is an essential part of learning.

True learning isn't complete until we have taken the time to debrief ourselves and reflect upon what was successful and why so we know when and how to use the same strategies again in the future. (You can read more about the power of reflection and self-assessment in my 2015 ASCD book *Teaching Students to Self-Assess*.)

Figure 3.2. Reflection Versus Self-Assessment

Reflection vs Self-Assessment

Reflection or Metacognition

- Thinking about thinking
- What was I expected to do?
- What was my process?
- What did I struggle with?
- How would I do things differently if I had another opportunity?

***Metacognition**: awareness and understanding of one's own thought processes or thinking about our own thinking

Self-Assessment

- What did I achieve with this experience and how does that align with the expectations?
- What level on the rubric is there evidence of in my learning?
- Or What success criteria have I been able to achieve and how do I know?

***Self-Assessment:** assessment or evaluation of oneself or one's actions and attitudes, in particular, of one's performance at a job or learning task considered in relation to an objective standard.

Source: Copyright Starr Sackstein. Used with permission.

**PERSPECTIVE: Lance Piantaggini,
High School Latin Teacher**

It took time, but years into my journey I tossed the proficiency-level rubrics out and settled on an expectations-based rubric. Rather than assess student proficiency levels, this set of criteria (i.e., the expectations) focused on the means or the *process* of developing that proficiency. I also started having students self-grade using these holistic rubrics, a major breakthrough in capturing students' voice. Students graded themselves, and then I just reviewed those evaluations.

Early on, the process was simple and straightforward. I would print the rubric (see Figure 3.3) and ask students to circle the level that corresponded to their self-assessment. Many students would circle the grade only, indicating that they were still focused on grades instead of learning, but I wasn't ready to see that yet.

It's important to note that I still did not provide feedback throughout this process except when students under- or overestimated their grades without any supporting evidence. That resulted in a short conversation about what the learning evidence was showing me and how it differed from what the student suggested. In those cases, I would change the grade and we would repeat the process the next quarter.

This all worked fine for several years, but fine is *just* fine. I was still missing one major piece of the puzzle: consistent feedback for all students. I did frequently refine my criteria and how I conveyed them on rubrics, and I would consistently point to posters showing what students were expected to do during the course (e.g., asking for clarification when they didn't understand something), but I was neglecting to hold students accountable throughout the grading term instead of just at the end of it. Furthermore, I was not doing much to help students meet expectations.

Figure 3.3. Latin Class Rubric and Expectations

Input Expectations Name_____ Date_____	
You exceed expectations, receiving <u>as much comprehensible input as you can</u> by <u>never</u> speaking over the teacher or class-mates, <u>always</u> asking when language is unclear, <u>never</u> missing class, and/or <u>always</u> reading independently! • *Why? How? You're always looking, listening, and asking at the highest level!*	95 (*A*)

You meet expectations, receiving <u>a lot of comprehensible input</u>.
 	
  • *Why? How? You're looking, listening, and asking!*
  • *What can you do to improve? Take it up a notch and <u>always</u> be on your game!*
	85 (*B*)

You <u>don't always</u> receive a lot of comprehensible input because you <u>sometimes</u> speak over the teacher and classmates, <u>sometimes</u> ask when language is unclear, <u>sometimes</u> are out of class or arrive late, and/or <u>sometimes</u> aren't reading independently.
 	
  • *Why? How? You sometimes look, listen, and ask, but time and energy are focused elsewhere.*
  • *What can you do to improve? Be more consistent with looking, listening, and asking.*
	75 (*C*)

You know what to do to receive comprehensible input, but <u>often don't meet expectations</u> because you speak over the teacher and classmates, don't ask when language is unclear, are often out of class, and/or aren't reading independently. The input you receive is <u>often not comprehensible</u>.
 	
  • *Why? How? You often don't look, listen, or ask. Your time is often focused elsewhere.*
  • *What can you do to improve? Listen a lot more, keep your phone away the whole class, and ask more questions when you're confused.*
	65 (*D*)

You <u>usually</u> don't meet expectations because you <u>frequently</u> speak over the teacher and classmates, <u>rarely</u> ask when language is unclear, are <u>frequently</u> out of class, and/or are <u>rarely</u> reading independently. Whatever input you receive is <u>almost always not comprehensible</u>. • *Why? How? You rarely look, listen, or ask. Your time and energy are usually focused elsewhere.* • *What can you do to improve? Start to listen, keep your phone away, and ask when confused.*	55 (*F*)
You speak over the teacher and classmates, allow language to be unclear, and/or aren't reading independently <u>so much</u> that you receive <u>almost no input</u>. • *Why? How? You almost never look, listen, or ask. Your time and energy are focused elsewhere.* • *What can you do to improve? See Mr. P. or Mr. Hawes for peer tutoring or enrollment in ACT.*	

Source: Courtesy of Lance Piantaggini. Used with permission.

Instead, my approach was to call students out when they were not meeting expectations. For example, if a student was talking over me, I would walk to the poster that said "Listen" on it, pause and patiently wait for them to stop talking, and then continue teaching. That was essentially the extent of my feedback.

Soon, my efforts shifted toward more intentional feedback (e.g., "This story is very clear, and the humorous ending is effective for the reader" or "I'm not sure what you meant here; could you clarify?"). I had been hesitant for so long to provide more input because the traditional kind of feedback in Latin classes—which I had experienced as a student myself— was hyper-focused on accuracy (e.g., correctly identifying verb tenses and uses). My attempts to avoid all that went pretty far in the opposite direction and were a far more productive approach for a second-language classroom.

> Once I went through this progression to arrive at grading expectations that aligned 1:1 with how students acquired language, I realized I could shift my feedback to this new process, straying from the more traditional language most teachers would offer.

Engaging with Peers to Enrich Student Understanding

We all know that group work and peer reviews are good for student learning, but too many of us abandon it when it doesn't work well the first or second time. Students will need a lot of guidance to collaborate effectively and provide one another with feedback. Getting students to engage in these ways is integral to helping them become more self-sufficient learners. It has clear benefits for both the person eliciting the help and the person providing it. Students have the opportunity to advocate and ask for the help they need as well as to collaborate with and support their peers by giving them feedback. Practicing finding and providing feedback can also help students improve their writing.

Peer engagement allows students to actively practice the skills and knowledge they need to master. It is an opportunity to get more ideas about what that learning can look like in an authentic way. Students can share how they approached the learning and their takeaways in ways teachers can't necessarily provide. When students approach a task together, they can tap into one another's knowledge and skills, bringing out the best in everyone. In well-designed group projects, students do more than just divide up the work; they collaborate to ensure that their learning is lining up throughout the process. And once students become experts in a particular area, other students learn whom to consult when they need improvement in that same area.

Using Portfolios to Track Growth

Seeing is believing, which is why portfolios are such a powerful way to track growth. Students who lack the vocabulary at first to discuss their growth can physically see their development over time by comparing earlier completed assignments to later ones. It is crucial to realize the value of having earlier examples of learning readily available to illustrate learning progress. Whether you are collecting hard copies of student work in a folder or using Google Drive or a tool like the MasteryBook, a portfolio serves as a map of growth.

Chapter Conclusions and Reflections

Goal setting and metacognition are potent tools that allow students to participate actively in their learning. Teaching students to be aware of where they are and where they are going provides a multitude of opportunities to differentiate their feedback and promote learning autonomy and partnership throughout the process. Learning is never a one-and-done or one-size-fits-all proposition. Our classrooms must mimic lifelong learning expectations that feed on error analysis, reflection, revision, and learning iteration.

Goal setting, feedback, and reflection will come up again and again in this book, as they are integral to successful student-led conferences and portfolios. As you reflect on the content of this chapter, consider the following questions:

- Who is setting goals for students in your class, and who is tracking them?
- What are you currently doing to ensure that all students have individualized learning plans that match their particular needs?
- What structures do you use for group work and student peer and self-assessment?
- Is metacognition a routine aspect of your classroom? If not, where will you start to add it? If so, how effective is it, and can you benefit from making it more structured?
- What are your biggest challenges with reflection and self-assessment?
- What does peer-to-peer interaction look like in your classes?

4

Developing a Portfolio System
That Supports Purposeful Goals

There is no more significant way to see the fruits of student labor than portfolio structures where students are in charge of tracking their learning growth. A portfolio is not just a place where we keep our learning; that would imply that they are a passive part of the learning process. If we allow them to only be that, they won't be nearly as functional as they can be.

This chapter explores what portfolios are and aren't and how to start developing effective portfolio systems in single classrooms, departments, schools, or even whole districts. With these systems in place, students will generate products that provide an accurate picture of their learning and the effectiveness of curricula.

According to Campus Press, the benefits of a portfolio for students and educators are as follows: "*For students*, digital portfolios foster independence while fueling reflection, creativity, and authentic lifelong learning. *For educators*, portfolio programs work wonders for tracking and assessing student growth and are an invaluable way to provide constructive feedback" (Burt & Morris, 2020).

Portfolios Defined

Ireland's National Council of Curriculum and Assessment (cited in EUfolio, 2015) defines e-portfolios as "student-owned dynamic digital workspaces wherein students can capture their learning and their ideas, access their collections of work, reflect on their learning, share it, set goals, seek feedback and showcase their learning and achievements" (p. 8). I would argue that this definition applies to hard-copy portfolios as well. We need to think of portfolios as "dynamic workspaces" rather than collections of finished work. Portfolios offer students abundant opportunities to reflect on their choices and learning, highlighting particular criteria in their selections and connecting their knowledge over time to show transfer and depth of understanding.

Variety of Kinds of Portfolios

Not all portfolios are created equal, so consider the different possibilities when deciding the portfolio you'd like your students to use (see Figure 4.1).

- **Capstone portfolios** are often used as a culminating project—something that students share after they have had the time to achieve a specific goal. Capstone projects allow students ownership of the topic and process, and a capstone portfolio is the living documentation of that process.

Figure 4.1. Types of Portfolios

Type	Description
Capstone	A culminating project demonstrating achievement of a specific goal
Achievement or Showcase	A demonstration of a learner's best efforts, including a clear reflection on why each piece has been selected
Progress or Growth	A collection of work showing a student's growth over time, with an explanation of how the process offered opportunity for growth
Professional	A collection of a variety of products reflecting professional work
Assessment	Used as a means of accountability to show evidence of learning
Hybrid	Any combination of portfolios

- **Achievement or showcase portfolios** are like capstones, but less focused on a single process. They showcase learners' best efforts and include a clear reflection on why each piece has been selected.
- **Progress or growth portfolios** are all about the process. They include work showing students' growth over time and students' explanations of how the process offered growth opportunities.
- **Professional portfolios** collect a variety of products reflecting professional work. For example, I maintain a hard-copy professional portfolio as a teacher that includes criteria and evidence I've collected.
- **Assessment portfolios** can be used as a means of accountability. Any of the portfolios mentioned above can be used in this way to show evidence of learning.
- **Hybrid portfolios** are any combination of the portfolios discussed above.

Perhaps you want students to show areas of growth and how they contrast with their showcase materials. For example, students may select artifacts that show growth in a particular skill through draft revisions in their writing and reflect on final showcase pieces that benefit from the earlier growth models. By doing so, they are demonstrating their learning journey by showing where they started, how they grew, and where they succeeded. It is up to the school or district to configure portfolios in a way that makes the most sense for assessment.

 PERSPECTIVE: Lisa Hicknell, Consultant, Ontario, Canada

In my classroom, we called our portfolios "learning journals," and they contained all the evidence of learning collected through the course. I used the Seesaw platform to house the journals after my daughter's kindergarten teacher introduced me to it. I was taken by the power of sharing learning with students and caregivers in real time. It wasn't something I'd ever known a high school teacher to do.

Every piece of evidence of learning went into the journal. All student products were housed there, as were elements of the process of completing them. All my feedback on student work, which followed Mark Barnes's (2015) SE2R feedback model from his book *Assessment 3.0*, was also included. The journal also contained evidence of learning from observations and conversations with the students. Students could also upload samples that they felt represented their learning and complete self-reflections after every significant learning activity. Anything that was entered into the learning journal was pegged to relevant standards.

Nothing in the portfolio was assigned a grade or level, and I didn't keep any records outside the learning journal; everything having to do with students' learning was transparent to them and their caregivers.

The wonderful thing about these portfolios is that they recorded student learning regardless of when or how it happened, so students didn't have to wait for an evaluation "event" to prove they knew something. As long as students showed up to class, even if they struggled to complete products, we could collaboratively document their learning so that there was always evidence to substantiate a grade. Parents and caregivers appreciated the portfolios being shared with them because they gave them a window into their child's learning that they don't normally get in high school.

Determining a Purpose

So, how should a teacher, school, or system determine the purpose of a portfolio? It depends on what they are using them for. It is essential to know your community so you can select the type of portfolio that will serve it best. You will also need to review state requirements and how best to fulfill them, especially if the portfolio is going to take the place of something more traditional. Consider the following questions:

- What are you hoping to achieve with this portfolio?
- What skills and content do you want students to demonstrate?
- Will the portfolio be assessed? If so, how?
- What criteria will show successful completion?

- What does exemplary work look like?
- What kind of variety will be acceptable?
- In what format should portfolios be submitted?
- Where will the portfolio be housed, and will it be digital or hard copy?
- Who will have access to the portfolio once it is created?
- How much autonomy does any individual teacher or student have when creating a portfolio?
- What kinds of buckets will students have to show learning? (Buckets are the overarching competencies in which multiple subject areas can fit.)
- What standards will be demonstrated through the portfolio?
- Will students need to present evidence of learning or just reflect on individual selections?
- What process will you use to teach students to "collect, select, reflect, connect"?

After asking these questions, it is crucial to backward-plan from what the successful candidate will contribute. What kinds of artifacts will show the success criteria as planned? How many different opportunities will they have to show that skill or knowledge in class? Once we know what we want our outcomes to be, it is easier to ensure that we are teaching for success. Teachers should ask, "What do kids know and what knowledge are they missing, and how will I fill the gaps?" Leaders should ask, "What do teachers know, and how much professional learning do we need to provide to ensure consistency if we are implementing portfolios together as a school or system?"

Co-Constructing Selection Criteria

Once you've identified a portfolio type and determined a purpose, you can start getting more granular. How do individual class objectives meet the needs of generic determined buckets, and how can you ensure students co-construct the portfolio selection criteria? (Remember, generic buckets are the larger competencies that all classes and content areas will fit in. They are "generic" because they don't get into specific standards.) Students will need to express the end goal of their portfolio first and then come up with a specific checklist to follow while deciding what to include.

Creating a Professional Portfolio as a Model

As I mentioned earlier, it is always helpful to complete an assessment you are asking students to do and identify any stumbling blocks they may encounter as well as making sure every step of the assignment is taught in advance. One way to ensure this is to create a professional portfolio that mirrors the kind of portfolio students are asked to create.

Portfolio Assessment Versus Traditional Testing

Standardized testing seeks to level the playing field for all students. Of course, most educators understand that such tests do nothing of the sort.

Standardized tests privilege the few who may be good at test taking or have the opportunity to work with tutors. Worse, they are often misleading and biased in favor of certain social and cultural experiences. (For example, when I took the New York State English Regents exam, one of the questions had to do with vaudeville, a long-outdated form of theatrical entertainment that students from other cultures might never even have heard of.) Other forms of testing would better illustrate the depth and understanding of student learning while also giving students more agency and decreasing their anxiety.

If educators genuinely want to know what students know and can do, they should have a universal portfolio system in place that allows students to gather evidence of learning over time. This can be implemented at the national or state level. Educators at every level should be included in the development process to devise the success criteria and the skill sets to be demonstrated over time. If we gather the right stakeholders to make sound decisions, all students will benefit.

Once criteria have been determined, students can start collecting learning from their earliest educational experiences. They can be issued an online account where work can be scanned and collected each year. This information can be shared with parents, students, and future teachers to help inform instruction. Rather than produce test scores that often don't highlight the depth of student learning, these online portfolios provide a more accurate picture of how students are doing.

Students can be taught to select work they are proud of for their portfolios and to express why they have selected it. Schools and/or states can determine how many pieces should be selected each year, and students can have ownership over what they believe best displays their learning. Obviously, teachers will be supporting students throughout this process.

After students make their selections, they should write standards-based reflections about what the pieces demonstrate and what they learned throughout the process. For younger students, teachers can and should provide feedback as well against standards. Because younger students won't necessarily understand how to do this right away, teachers should scaffold the process a little longer and adjust the language of the standards to be more kid-friendly. Then the feedback they provide on students' selections will be in a language the students understand, ensuring they'll be able to progressively do more on their own as the year goes on.

At the end of each school year, students should discuss the goals they've set and met as well as new goals to be worked on in the following year. Students can learn the language to use for these discussions at a young age. In the goals, students should talk about the areas where they see progress and then decide what they want to work on moving forward.

Each content area should have a subfolder in the portfolio. In addition to content-specific goals and learning related to academics, students should also be able to demonstrate interpersonal skills like communication, collaboration, and self-regulation. Rubrics can be developed to help students assess their learning levels. Graduation criteria, as well as college- and career-readiness criteria, should also be included.

One high school I taught at used to have exit presentations where students had to defend their learning and express why they felt they were ready for their next learning journey. Instead of testing, consider implementing these presentations at the end of each school year. Students will get comfortable sharing what they have learned and asking questions to help clarify that learning. Students, teachers, and leaders can sit on the panels during these presentations. Throughout the school year, students can be taught to lead their conferences, and their parents can sit with them to review the portfolio work. Advisory teachers should be there to provide support, too. In the younger grades, where there is only one teacher, students should be included in the conferences and not left at home. It is important that conversations about learning be conducted with the learner present.

Learning is nuanced, and assessment should be, too. Be sure to offer students the opportunity to be seen as whole people who can demonstrate different skills and knowledge in many ways over time.

PERSPECTIVE: Katie Harrison, Science Coordinator and Portfolio Committee Leader

The closure of schools and the transition to a completely virtual learning environment during the COVID-19 pandemic, then the transition back from virtual to concurrent the following year, turned our system on its head in a lot of ways, especially as it relates to grading practices. Our district collected everyday evidence—that is, an assignment completed and assessed daily—as part of an accountability system for both learning and attendance. Retaking and redoing work was now required practice in secondary classrooms. We pivoted to a holistic rubric for assigning course grades, and teachers did everything in their power to ensure that students were as successful as they could be in completing courses during those two academic years.

As my district transitioned out of the 2020–2021 school year, the grading committee generated a five-year plan for shifting from a traditional grading system to a portfolio-based system by 2024–2025. The new plan called for the following strategies:

- Redistributing the weighting of summative and formative assessments from 80/20 to 90/10 and moving away from a 100-point scale to a 4-point system
- Continuing the retake/redo practices (those practices aligned by assessment over time to ensure that students have multiple opportunities to show learning after feedback has been provided)
- Ensuring that no student received a grade lower than 50 percent in any marking period
- Separating behavior and academic reporting on the report card

- Piloting portfolio-based systems for grading within select departments
- Training all departments on the portfolio-based system
- Implementing a portfolio-based system and holistic rubric for final assignments

Every summer, I work with teachers to lay the groundwork for the next academic year. In the summer of 2021, our focus was on curriculum alignment, learning targets, and student metacognition. I built out unit maps for as many courses as I could, with teachers in charge of the courses. We discussed such issues as student achievement, what an *A* grade looks like, feedback, redoing and resubmitting work, reflection, and assessment. To drive these conversations, I used quotes from experts rather than my own words.

That summer and in the early days of the new school year, I worked to amass a group of 21 science teachers and 3 instructional coaches who were ready to learn more about portfolios and were interested in field-testing this work. The district assistant superintendent afforded me time and money to work with Starr on training these teachers and coaches to start the next steps of our transition to portfolios.

After some reflection, I realized that I was about to make a major mistake if I continued with the plan we had developed. The secondary grading plan was for all secondary courses, not just secondary science, and I didn't want the perception to be that because I'm the science coordinator, this was just meant for "my people." I realized I was about to embark on a journey that other departments may not like. There was a high probability that what worked for us in science, from language to rubrics, would not necessarily translate to other content areas. (Don't believe me? Ask those who don't teach science about dealing with data or modeling!) The last thing I wanted to do was create a different portfolio requirement for each major content area. This would not have been beneficial for students or families, as it would have created too much varying language and too many new expectations, which would make an already new process even more confusing.

So, I went back to the drawing board. The assistant superintendent and I came up with Plan B: Starr would work with me and the other coordinators and specialists to define what a portfolio is and generate a list of basic requirements for it—what we called "Skills Buckets"—as a foundation for moving forward (see Figure 4.2). It took six sessions and several months working with Starr, some of which were remarkably painful, to develop these elements as well as to start creating a portfolio handbook for the district. (You can see the table of contents for Starr's school in Figure 12.1 on p. 145.)

Next, we needed to generate a timeline for the full portfolio development and training lift. We also cultivated a larger group of teachers than our original leadership planning committee to build out a subgroup of the grading committee called the Portfolio Workgroup (PWg). Initially, this workgroup was open to volunteers from all district secondary schools and departments. It was imperative for us to create a safe space for teachers where grading and assessment practices could be talked about freely. (In preceding years, conversations about grading practices had become contentious, and the changes that COVID-19 forced on the system made it a sore subject.) The workgroup was encouraged to garner feedback from others, too, and administrators and counselors were invited to join the work later to apply their perspectives. We knew that transparency was the only way this initiative would succeed and stand the test of time. The portfolio development and implementation program included a communication plan separate from the development of the process in order to ensure clear updates and public-facing documents for clarity as well as present opportunities to garner feedback from stakeholders throughout the process.

Initially, the PWg consisted of 35 members across the middle and high school grades and multiple content areas. Our first four meetings revolved around refining the portfolio's Skills Buckets. Those sessions also offered

Figure 4.2. Portfolio Buckets

"Bucket"	Explanation of the Bucket
Argumentation	I can gather evidence through research and analysis.
	I can evaluate sources for credibility and perspectives offered in my research and analysis.
	I can explain concepts through the synthesis, application, and sharing of ideas using evidence to support my argument.
Communication	I can express knowledge, ideas, and concepts using the appropriate output strategy and content relevant to my course and grade level.
	I can further discuss information, ideas, and evidence (including relevant data) with my peers in collaborative ways to help their learning and my own.
	I can present this information to an authentic audience in effective ways when asked.
Constructing Solutions	I can use and analyze information gathered through the course and my own research and/or analysis to • Solve problems, • Plan and execute ideas, and/or • Represent concepts with student-generated models.
Innovation	I can demonstrate metacognitive thinking, synthesis across content areas, and originality in my work to creatively solve problems or present new solutions.
	I can choose the appropriate tools and resources to produce that work to demonstrate my learning.

Source: Courtesy of Katie Harrison. Used with permission.

opportunities to capture questions and concerns that teachers had about our work and the transition. We finalized the buckets toward the end of the school year, then continued our work in a summer professional learning session. That session was an opportunity for PWg members to dig into the Skills Buckets through their own content-area lens and to edit the draft portfolio handbook. By August 2022, we had a district definition of portfolios, the Skills Buckets (a.k.a. course competencies), and a draft handbook as a foundation to resume the work in the fall.

The PWg defined a *portfolio* as a purposeful, systemic process for collecting, evaluating, and showcasing student progress toward attainment of learning goals. The portfolio contains artifacts of student work that exemplify students' current ability to apply relevant knowledge and skills to reflections about the selected pieces.

The work-in-progress folder is a collection of all work completed or in progress in every grade and every course (including both high-stakes projects and informal assignments) maintained on Google Drive. If items are completed on paper, photos are uploaded to the platform. (Note that *not* all work in this folder will end up in the final presentation or course-end portfolio.)

At the end of each course, students will be expected to have a finished portfolio that represents the work they completed across the term to demonstrate their proficiency in relevant standards. This course-based information stays in students' portfolios until the following year, when they continue to build on their learning and are provided opportunities to continue the standards loop and/or expand for each subject, as most skills and content in classes develop more as they continue through a progression of courses. So we want to ensure that all new learning builds on prior learning.

Examples of work that can be included with reflections in students' portfolios include projects, formal essays, labs, slide presentations, articles, other media (e.g., broadcasts, music videos, photographs, InDesign layouts), field trip analyses, and so on.

Until the start of the 2022–2023 academic year, the PWg guidelines were more theoretical than practical. One major struggle we faced was that everyone wanted examples of what they were supposed to be doing. But no one had done this work on a large scale across all secondary schools and grade levels in a district simultaneously before. I had read publications by Starr Sackstein, Cathy Vatterott, Thomas Guskey, Jay McTighe, Robert Marzano, Susan Blum, John Hattie, Joe Feldman, and Susan Brookhart; surfed countless articles online from sources such as *Edutopia,* ASCD, *Phi Delta Kappan,* and Learning Forward; viewed countless YouTube videos and TED Talks; and followed individuals on Twitter like Tyler Rablin and Monte Syrie. All these resources spoke to me. All of them offered nuggets of information that I have used and will continue to use in talking about assessing the learning of students in ways that are equitable and reflective of their learning. But none discussed setting up systems in multiple middle and high schools and across all subjects.

The next steps of this work involved "the lift": collecting standards, rubrics, student exemplars, and other materials that lend themselves to field-testing the second half of the year, providing a solid foundation for portfolio growth.

This past school year, the PWg expanded to 54 members, including administrators, counselors, and coaches, and we began grappling with assessment matrices and course standard matrices. While all our courses will be held accountable for meeting the same competencies, each course will have its own set of portfolio standards that students will be held accountable for meeting. During our third meeting of the year, I realized that we needed some time to meet face-to-face instead of online and an extended window of time to grapple with courses and their nuances to generate templates for future portfolio development.

> The next step for us to take will be identifying the needs of each individual department. I will be meeting with my director to share those needs, and we will work together on a plan for the continued development of the portfolio for all courses while implementing the field testing that will be occurring this spring. Once the field test is complete, we will gather the feedback generated from this process to further refine the portfolio handbook and to update the timelines for our next steps.

Katie's district is working hard to put a system in place that promotes equity and voice for students and consistency and clarity for teachers. I've been fortunate enough to help Katie and her team avoid the pitfalls I experienced in my own school. In our case, we were a much smaller team making decisions for the whole. This is something that Katie has made sure isn't the case in her district as she tries to make decisions as authentic and organized and collaborative as possible.

In your school or district, you will want a creation and implementation period that explores how your school will define portfolios, build specific competency buckets that will work across content areas, and then build out content-specific alignment to those buckets. Katie's district is doing that with a series of matrices and single-point rubrics. You will also want to test out what you put in place with a pilot group who will be ready to make revisions before it goes into the whole group. Ultimately, structures will need to be as clear as possible so that expectations are consistent across classrooms, content areas, and buildings. This is how we create equity for our kids.

As you go through this process, remember that implementation will take a minimum of two to three years depending on the size of your community, which will need to be informed and educated about what you are doing, why you are doing it, and how it will impact student learning. Katie's district created a workgroup for communicating to both internal and external stakeholders. To ensure that the language they use is consistent and clear, buy-in is optimal, and spin is minimal, they are also consulting with their district's communication expert.

Chapter Conclusions and Reflections

There are many ways to successfully use portfolios, so teams must determine which ways they want to use theirs and what form they will take. Katie's district came up against many challenges but also received a wealth of ideas from teachers who have participated in the process so far.

In this chapter, we described what a portfolio is along with the variety of types and purposes. As you read this chapter, I hope you considered the benefits and potential challenges of portfolios as well as how to use the challenges to bring more clarity into the process. Building a portfolio system takes time, and creating a handbook for your school may be one way to ensure consistency and professional learning for your staff.

As you reflect on the content of this chapter, consider the following questions:

- What will be the purpose of your portfolios?
- What type of portfolio will best line up with that purpose?
- What role will students have in the process of creation?
- How will you communicate with your community about this shift?
- What kinds of professional learning will you and/or your team need to be successful?
- What pitfalls are you worried about?
- What are some potential areas of pushback, and how can you frontload information to avoid them?
- Have you created a sample portfolio yet?
- What portfolio system will you create or use?
- Who are your allies in this process?
- What roles will different members of your team play?
- Are you able to use a portfolio in lieu of a final exam or as a graduation requirement?

Part 2

Developing Conferring Protocols

Now that you have a culture of learning in place and students have the vocabulary and clarity necessary to track and discuss their learning through their portfolios, it's time to dive into the conferring protocols you will use to ensure your time is spent well. Teachers are keen to ask probing questions and have a good idea of what we expect kids to know and be able to do in our learning spaces. The real challenge is handing over control of this process to the students.

This section starts with modeling practices. As we model the conferencing process for students, deliberately showing them how we talk about learning, students become more adept at doing so themselves. We then move from modeling to active practice and partnering using gradual release of responsibility. We also consider shared feedback and mutual discussion around learning throughout the formative assessment process.

As you read through this section, consider the following questions:

- What content am I teaching, and how will I show students how best to engage in formative assessment?
- What do I currently do well, and where do I need additional strategies?
- How do I elicit feedback from students to ensure I'm meeting their needs?
- Is my classroom a place where students feel they can advocate for their own learning? What evidence do I have to support my claim here?

5

Putting Protocols in Place
to Ensure Success

Any successful experience starts with some structure in place to ensure clarity and as little variance as possible. However, classrooms are anything but predictable given the number of personalities in them and the sheer volume of moving parts. For this reason, protocols have the potential to help students achieve success. Students need structures that help them through new experiences, and the predictability of a protocol or routine makes it easier for students to focus on meeting goals. In this chapter, we explore how to develop protocols and routines to ensure the success of portfolios and student-led conferences in your unique learning spaces.

Getting Started with Modeling and Metacognition

A routine will only take hold if you model it using metacognition. When you first begin to demonstrate a learning process to students, consider a think-aloud while you're walking them through it, explaining what is going on, why it is happening, and what the benefits to the structure are. You may even consider sharing the different ways you could have approached different aspects of the protocol to ensure students understand there isn't only one right way to do things.

Another effective modeling strategy is a fishbowl. This is when teachers or students model the routine or protocol in real time in the center of the classroom while the rest of the class gathers around and watches.

It is easy enough to prepare for a fishbowl. First, consider the strategy you want to model. If you are fortunate enough to have a second adult in the room, you can model with them. Better yet, if you have two students who are adept at the strategy, have them do the modeling. Set them up in the middle of the classroom and have them literally demonstrate for the rest of the class. It can be helpful to record the fishbowl and use it as a reference for the future. (An example of a fishbowl I conducted with my co-teacher modeling how to get the most out of literature circles can be found at www.youtube.com/watch?v=wALGs-xop4Y&t=118s.) Video examples help students to see exactly what they will be doing; you can then offer them opportunities to ask questions and imagine alternative ways of being successful.

Developing a Process That Works

These days, small class sizes are a novelty. If you work in a city system as I did, the norm is a class of 30 students or more. This year, most of my classes are maxed out at 34. When there are this many students in each class, the idea of conducting classroom conferences can feel daunting at best. Here are some ways to ensure time in a full classroom is indeed spent talking to students about their learning with minimal out-of-class commitments:

- Select a week when students will be engaged in some kind of project-based learning that requires little to no direct instruction in the classroom. You can still administer a minilesson if necessary, but really try to plan so that student conferences coincide with work time (preferably at midterm and also at the end of the term). You will be meeting with individual students throughout the semester, of course, but not as formally as you are planning to now. The rest of the class should be engaged in meaningful group or independent work while you are talking to individual students.
- Develop a Google form that will help you prepare students for the time they will sit with you. Students should be prepared to talk during the conference, and ongoing reflection should be expected.
- Since students will be prepared for the discussion, you can plan to set aside a certain amount of time during class for that. Make sure the Google forms are filled out at least one day prior to the conference.
- Give students at least a week to complete the forms so they have time to really think about what they write.

- Read the students' forms before you sit down with them. It's easiest to set a schedule based on which students completed the form first and go in that order.
- Jot down things you notice or highlight them on the form if you have questions after your initial read-through. When you speak with students, try to mention at least one thing you noticed in their form so they know you read what they wrote.
- Make the conference schedule public so students know when it's their turn and transition time can be minimized. I like to post it on the whiteboard. For the year's first round of conferences, I email the schedule out, but the reminder up on the board is helpful even with the email.
- Stick to the plan as much as possible. Your goal is to obtain answers to any questions you may have. In my preconference email, I let kids know exactly what to expect. For example, they should tell me what they are most proud of and why, where they are most improved and what level of proficiency they have reached, and what evidence they have for improvement. Sometimes I also like to ask them what one goal is moving forward that we can start working on.
- If you tend to lose track of time, use a timer to move through the conferences efficiently.
- Keep a list of what students say during conferences and add your own notes. This information can serve as evidence for subsequent conversations with parents or administrators.
- Make sure students keep track of what they say as well. Teaching learners to be responsible for their feedback ensures they can effectively meet goals and track growth. This will make reflections more meaningful and learning more focused.
- Late or missing students who didn't complete their forms go last, as their sessions are likely to last longer than the others. You may consider setting up their appointments during lunch or before or after school to ensure privacy, but no student gets out of having these conferences.

Once the conferences have been completed, there should be no surprises come report card time. Students know what is going on, and so do parents. These conversations keep learning transparent, and progress is always in the open. Making sure that students understand where their mastery level is and what needs improvement ensures continued growth and focus in the upcoming term. It also helps you to differentiate learning better among students.

Reviewing and Revising Practices to Optimize Time

The forms have been filled out, and the appointment schedule has been emailed. Now it's time to prepare.

I meet with my students multiple times a year during extended project time in class to check in on their progress. In the "no grades" classroom, student conversations about learning are a must. Whether these discussions are formal or informal, students must be getting focused feedback all the time.

As I prepare for the class time being spent knee to knee, I like to review the body of student work I have for each child. If I plan on meeting with seven students a day (two before school starts, one in newspaper class, and then four during class), I like to make sure to review their form answers, my feedback on their documents, and any questions they may have asked through social media or an online tool like email, Google Docs, or LMS.

It's tempting for a teacher to use a full 10 minutes to tell students what they're doing wrong or what needs improvement, but that's not what these conferences are about. Rather, they are about discussing what students deem most important about their goals and progress. The more involvement and ownership students have in their learning, the more invested they are in seeing it through to the end; teachers are just a support mechanism to help them do so.

I start each conference as follows: "What do you feel you have improved upon and are doing well now?" Then I ask, "What would you like to work on now, and how can I help you?" We've been using this vocabulary since the beginning of the year, and the standards are extremely transparent, so students know what they are having a hard time with and can articulate that to me. Then, I can help them develop a plan that can be measured and followed to keep them accountable for their own progress.

Regardless of what I consider to be a student's greatest challenge, it is important for me to let them lead the conferences so as not to overwhelm them. I'm here to offer solutions and keep the conversation on track. No "stinkin' thinkin'" or negative self-talk—anything students want to improve, they can, with practice. My job is to provide them with opportunities to surmount the challenges they face.

After our 10 minutes are up, students should walk away with solid goals that will be tracked through the next few projects. I will provide them with continual check-ins and help until the training wheels can come off.

There is nothing more gratifying than seeing a student who knows they get it and can recognize their own growth and be able to articulate it to another person. Bearing witness to these moments—and serving as the mirror students need to see themselves—is my greatest honor as a teacher.

PERSPECTIVE: Emma Chiappetta, Instructional Coach and Math Teacher (Part 2)

My class structure is designed with conferencing in mind. Three out of four class meeting times each week are dedicated to self-paced work and conferences. The fourth day is devoted to problem solving in groups (in the style of Peter Liljedahl's *Building Thinking Classrooms in Mathematics, Grades K–12* [2020]). Self-pacing makes conferences extremely manageable. It means I don't have every student in the class asking for a conference on the same day. It also means that students know exactly what they should do each class period.

In my class, each learning module starts with a standard. I give students a menu of learning options they can use to acquire the necessary knowledge and context for understanding that standard. Options might include videos, textbook readings, guided exploration activities, or pattern recognition exercises. Students choose at least one option from the menu. Next, they apply their skills by choosing from another variety of options: online problem-solving databases, textbook problems, worksheets, quiz games, and so on. When they feel they have the learning down, students ask to take a short summative quiz or complete an application task for which I provide feedback. After that, if they feel ready, we conference. Figure 5.1 demonstrates the process for determining whether students are ready and how the process will work.

Figure 5.1. Formative Assessment and the Conference Process

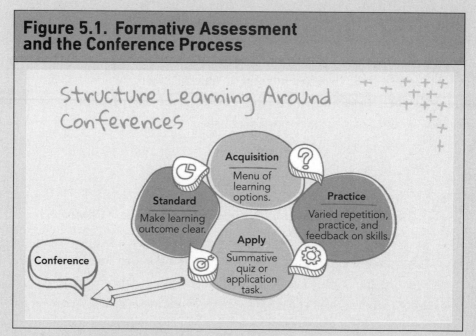

Source: Courtesy of Emma Chiappetta. Used with permission.

To ensure that conferences go smoothly, students are prepared, and each student is evaluated equitably, I design a list of need-to-know questions that I make sure to ask at every conference. To create the list, I begin by breaking down the standard into bullet points and creating at least one question per bullet. From there, I identify the questions that students really need to be able to answer. I also plan a few extension questions or scaffolding questions to probe students who seem stuck.

Before finalizing the list, I check that the questions are aligned with all the practice material I've provided. Finally, I prepare myself to be flexible. A student may demonstrate mastery in ways that I can't predict: a question, a drawing, a reflection—any of these might be enough to signal mastery. Figure 5.2 shows the process I go through to determine which categories

Putting Protocols in Place to Ensure Success

Figure 5.2. Conference "Need-to-Knows"

Standards	xxx	Break down into bullet points and create a question for each bullet point.
Priorities	xxx	Determine which questions are "need to knows."
Extensions	xxx	Plan additional questions extending beyond "need to knows."
Scaffolds	xxx	Plan probing questions to elicit information from students that they might not think they know.
Alignment	xxx	Make sure the learning tools, practice, and summative quiz all align with the questions you plan to add.
Flexibility	xxx	What are all the different ways that "mastering" this standard could look?

Note: The *X*s indicate how many pieces of evidence successfully demonstrate the category once you've determined what each of the categories will encompass. Teachers will be able to look for a quick understanding of what students know and where they need to keep offering learning opportunities.
Source: Courtesy of Emma Chiappetta. Used with permission.

and questions I will ask and then how I indicate how many demonstrations they show, indicated by the boldface *X*s.

The following list is a sequence of questions I ask during conferences with my statistics class. In this class, my students were exploring a standard related to scatter plots and linear regression.

- When might you use a scatter plot?
- Can you draw one? Make sure to label it with two appropriate variables.
- Describe the scatter plot using the vocabulary you've been learning.
- Estimate and interpret the correlation coefficient for your plot.

- Draw a line of best fit and come up with the equation for it.
- Interpret the slope and intercept of the line of best fit.
- Show me the data you've been using for your project. Which variables would be interesting to compare using a scatter plot?
- Use Google Sheets to make a scatter plot and add the line of best fit. Interpret it. What does this actually mean in terms of the variables you chose?

Because I run a self-paced classroom on conference days, all my resources are designed so that students can work without me. They set goals for each class period at the beginning of the week and refer to their goal sheets to figure out what they need to do. I always check in with the class between conferences to answer questions and see how they're doing. I also usually face the class while I'm in a conference so that I can quickly glance to see if anyone is having an issue. If I see students off task, a lighthearted comment like "Kian, are you bored? Can I get you something more interesting to do?" can help.

To make sure that the conferences fairly assess all students equally, I only evaluate student answers to "need to know" questions, even if I ask side questions that are inspired by the students' curiosity. Some teachers have expressed concerns about other students in the class hearing the questions before I conference with them or copying the answers their peers provide. To combat this, I always have the student with whom I am conferencing use a mini-whiteboard to generate a problem that they will then solve, create their own drawing, or use their own data set to demonstrate a skill. This way, each conference is unique.

If I'm prepared with my questions and students are prepared with the requisite knowledge, conferences usually go really smoothly and efficiently. Because my class is self-paced, meeting times are usually naturally spaced out. I try not to do more than three conferences per class period so that I also have time for opening, closing, and checking in between conferences.

Students never "fail" a conference. I have had conferences where both the student and I quickly realize they are not prepared. In those cases, the conference turns into a formative conversation. I answer questions, make the expectations clear, and provide the student with additional resources or practice opportunities.

Finally, some teachers wonder whether conferencing is a rigorous enough strategy for tracking and assessing performance in math. The answer is "Absolutely!" During the conference, students need to not only demonstrate that they can apply the same skills they would need to demonstrate on a test, but also explain how and why they are executing a step in a certain way. They need to understand the context of the skills they are using, especially if I ask them to generate their own examples. After talking about the content, students tend to understand it at a deeper level and retain the knowledge longer than they would after a traditional test.

Chapter Conclusions and Reflections

This chapter explored a variety of ways to set up protocols for seamlessly including student-led conferences in class. There is no one right way to set up conferencing, and I can't emphasize enough how much your students' specific personalities will affect the decisions you make. Making sure to have structures in place for breaking down complicated ideas will greatly benefit you and your students. Ideally, schools should set up systems that promote portfolio and conference time as a part of regular scheduling so that teachers don't feel like it is an "extra" or that they don't have enough time to go deep enough to make the structures meaningful.

As you reflect on the content of this chapter, consider the following questions:

- What protocols are working well in your class right now? Can they be repurposed or revised?
- What are your go-to strategies for modeling new protocols and learning?
- How do you know whether the strategies are successful?
- How much does student voice factor into that understanding?

6

Partnering with Students in the Formative Process

In this chapter, we explore the benefits of partnering with students intentionally to bring them into the formative assessment process. It is no longer the role of the teacher to merely make a plan and then execute it; that will take us only so far. If we want students to own their learning, then we must partner with them, not just in theory but in practice, and ensure that voices in the learning environment are informing the choices we make as a team.

Student Self-Advocacy and Assessment for Learning

Think about your own approach to learning. When you don't know how to do something, do you immediately throw your hands up in the air and admit defeat? I surely hope not. Think of the experiences and learning you would miss out on if you took that approach. Too often, our students quit before they get very far because we don't ask them to persevere and their threshold for productive struggle is lower than it needs to be. Ironically, many of these same students will persevere time and again when they fail a level in a video game. Have you ever asked yourself why students demonstrate this tenacity in gaming but not in learning? It may have to do with ownership and interest. Why not ask them? See what they say, then see if you can apply those answers to helping them persevere with classroom learning. Then, encourage students to set meaningful SMART (Specific, Measurable, Attainable, Relevant, Time-bound) goals with an accompanying action plan that lets them know when they need support and whom to reach out to for it.

As different children call for my attention over the course of the day, I notice the ones who don't ask at all. Usually, these are the students who actually need the most help. I also notice how paralyzed students become when help isn't imminent. Many teachers, like parents, struggle with allowing students to work through the learning process without offering "help." In fact, many students have been enabled for so long they don't know how to initiate learning without following explicit steps that have been given to them. This can have a terrible effect on student learning.

Unfortunately, the learning process has been systematically dismantled by traditional schooling, which has forced students to avoid thought and mindlessly complete tasks that become less and less meaningful over time. When these students encounter a real challenge that requires problem solving and following multiple steps, they need to relearn how to learn. Here are some tips for breaking students out of this helpless loop and into a more self-motivated and self-aware learning state:

- Remind students that what they think matters and they need to trust themselves when it comes time to learn. This lesson will take time and some confidence building to take root.
- Encourage students to practice taking risks. They don't need to have the "right" answers to grow in their learning. They need to take chances and learn from the outcomes, discerning between solutions that work and those that don't.
- When students make suggestions, take them seriously and, whenever possible, integrate them into the learning process. If you are going to ask students to trust themselves, you need to trust them, too, and to show it with your actions.
- Teach students to meaningfully reflect on their process at the beginning, middle, and end of their learning. Give them cues to help them navigate and track their own progress against standards, and give them time both in and out of class to further practice the learning process.
- Use these reflections to set a few SMART goals that provide actions to be taken both immediately and over time, where the focus can be made more personal in the process. Because teachers are taking the pulse of the whole class, using individual student reflections allows the teacher to ensure teachers and students

are on the same page regarding which goals matter. Use these goals to help students grow as learners.

• Always remind students to try several different approaches to something before asking for help. They need some productive struggle and problem-solving time before they can figure out that they can't figure something out.

• Be a safety net, but not the first line of defense. I always remind students that this is *their* learning experience now; I graduated from high school a long time ago. My job is to grow as a practitioner and develop better relationships to ensure they are getting what they need without me robbing them of their own aha moments.

• Be patient. It may take longer than you would like for students to claim the incredible freedom you are offering them. This doesn't mean they don't want it, just that they don't know what to do with it yet. Being in control of our learning is a tremendous opportunity and responsibility, and some students may not know how to deal with that at first. They will learn if given enough time, though.

• Give students the opportunity to ask for help when it is necessary. Don't ask them repeatedly if they need it but, rather, create an environment that invites a confident student to know when it is time to ask.

Once students accept the power of their own learning, they understand how to get their needs met, how to distinguish between wanting help and needing it, and when it is appropriate to ask for support. As teachers, we need to help students hone this self-awareness so that they can better self-advocate during the learning process—not waiting until it is too late, but also not asking prematurely.

PERSPECTIVE: Bonnie Nieves, High School Science Teacher and Founder of Educate on Purpose Consulting

I've found that the best way to promote self-advocacy is to encourage students to reflect on their learning using prompts that scaffold deepening metacognitive processes. I start each year using exit tickets that ask students to write down what they learned from a lesson and what problem they might be able to solve with that knowledge. (Each of the following items can be used as its own exit ticket, or several of them may be combined as one exit ticket, depending on what you are assessing.)

- Explain something you learned in class last week.
- What problem might a person with that knowledge be able to solve?
- Set a goal for this week.
- List two strategies that will help you accomplish it.

I provide feedback that encourages students to dig deeper into their learning process. This feedback is specific to the goal of each student. Here are some examples:

- Setting goals is an integral part of improving.
- Why did you choose that goal?
- Can you tell me more about that goal?
- Do you have similar goals in other classes?

After a few weeks of practice, students begin to write entries in their journals to evaluate their performance on assignments and any changes they might make for next time. I then have students review previous entries and write a reflection on what they notice about their own learning.

We demonstrate the importance of collaborative learning by discussing various learning strategies students have tried and curating a class strategy bank. This helps me visualize each student's learning process so that I can begin to provide knowledge acquisition and demonstration options that meet the needs of all students. The composition of journal entries begins to change as students see the value of their work. Themes evolve as students experience the satisfaction of learning new things, being able to transfer knowledge, applying their learning in authentic ways, and teaching other people.

Students take ownership of their learning and find personally meaningful reasons to participate in class. Their reflections highlight their intrinsic sense of accomplishment rather than the extrinsic motivation of grades.

After modeling, practicing, and sharing a variety of reflection, self-awareness, and self-management strategies, students are prepared for meaningful goal setting. At the launch of each new unit, I provide them with learning objectives and facilitate conversations with prompts such as these:

- Why do people need to know this?
- What can someone do with this knowledge?
- Where might we learn more about this?

These questions empower students to set content goals for themselves and create their own rubrics. Each student decides their goal for the next unit based on what interests them most about the learning objectives. We use a sample rubric as a model to determine how students want to be evaluated, and students write their criteria for success. Finally, students use the following prompts to design their learning plans: "How will you know if you are not progressing toward your goal?" and "What perseverance strategy will you use when faced with a challenge?"

As much as I focus on the process of learning and the importance of taking risks in the interest of growing and exploring new ideas, there are always going to be students who prioritize grades over all else. Their goals tend to include things like "get better grades," "pay more attention in class," and "make the honor roll," and their milestones are progress reports. In these cases, I remind students of the long-term goals they have talked about (e.g., becoming a doctor or a millionaire). I ask them to think about how any single score will help them achieve that goal and consider whether the skills they employ to reach goals and recover from setbacks are the most valuable aspects of the process.

I am confident that taking the time to integrate motivation, reflection, and empathy is essential to forming a long-term relationship with learning and that knowledge is more permanent when connected to a meaningful experience.

Empowering Student Leaders to Support the Learning Community

Once students become adept at self-advocacy, it is easier to empower them to lead differently throughout the learning community. You can easily identify the students who stand out in different areas and utilize their unique approaches to learning and topics to enrich the overall learning environment. Cultures that empower students create authentic and inclusive experiences for learning that transcend the content and skills being taught and can more readily be transferred to scenarios for advocacy in the future.

One way I used student leadership successfully in my humanities classes was by creating expert groups that helped maintain student ownership and advocacy throughout the year. By training individual students and small student groups with particular skill sets, I successfully created an environment where students sought one another out instead of coming to the teacher first, lessening the lift for me. Additionally, students were better able to identify where they needed help and on what, and since they knew where to get the help they needed, they could usually keep going without my prompting. (You can learn more about student expert groups in my 2017 ASCD book *Peer Feedback in the Classroom*.)

Gaining Feedback from Students to Improve Instruction

It is not enough for students to receive feedback from their teacher and from one another; teachers should regularly elicit feedback from their students about their learning in classes, too. The more we know what students are truly getting out of the learning, the better we can plan for the unique makeup of our classes each year. Students can provide valuable feedback on pacing, activity variety, and the level of texts. However, such feedback will only be successful if we are receptive and use it to improve the culture and learning environment. It also makes sense to acknowledge the feedback and directly point out when it has a positive effect on your practice. Creating an ongoing dialogue with students about their learning keeps us focused and flexible.

After a unit (and throughout where appropriate), I would formally and informally survey students to garner feedback on my instructional approach. These surveys took the form of digital polls or invitations for conversations that extended beyond what we discussed in class.

Each piece of student feedback I received provided insight that helped me adjust and revise the process to ensure greater success in the future. The feedback also helped me understand what was working and what practices I needed to lean into more frequently and with greater intentionality. Feedback from students helped elevate their voices in our day-to-day learning. Following are some examples of feedback I received from students in surveys about their work in peer expert groups:

> Being in groups has both helped and gotten in the way of my creativity, depending on the situation. I've learned to adapt to people's various personalities and strengths so that we can produce work that reflects all our skills. Sometimes, the people who were most willing to complete a certain assignment were the ones who ended up doing most of the work. In these cases, I was brought out of my comfort zone to take on unfamiliar roles. I'm usually the type to internalize my thoughts and feelings and write them down rather than express them aloud, but being in groups has pushed me to grow as a reader, speaker, and writer. Working in groups has also helped me learn more about interpersonal dynamics and develop my patience and openness to other people's ideas.

> Working in groups, I learned that everyone has different standards. Some members might think the assignment or project is fine to turn in, but I don't think it's "perfect" until it's been finished well.

> It's been challenging to work in groups that have pushed me to take on roles that I would otherwise avoid, but this challenge has improved my writing. I now qualify my arguments instead of staying stuck in a single way of thinking. Different group members bring diverse personalities and perspectives, and I try to capture this complexity in my writing.

> Working in groups has led me to understand the different approaches people take to complete assignments. This understanding helps me to understand myself better and question my own perspective and methods. I have become able to adapt to groups and understand what we're able to produce, what might be beyond our ability, what we are willing to commit to, and whether we need to switch roles. I don't have a very forceful personality—I provide feedback pretty diplomatically—but

occasionally, if I see someone disengaged from the assignment, I will become more assertive. Usually, though, I provide suggestions that create a collaborative setting where everyone feels eager to participate.

Chapter Conclusions and Reflections

Student self-advocacy is a big part of the personalized learning experience. As we empower students to know themselves as learners, we create opportunities for them to ask better questions and garner the help they need from their peers and teachers. Portfolios and student-led conferences open the door to a deeper understanding of learning and a greater partnership between educators and learners. This chapter explored ways you can help students learn to advocate for their learning as well as ways to elicit feedback from students to ensure their voices make a difference.

As you reflect on the content of this chapter, consider the following questions:

- What role do your students play in the formative assessment process in your classroom or school?
- Do students currently advocate for their learning? What does it look like?
- Are there areas where you can release more control and create an atmosphere for student advocacy?
- Do you invite student feedback to improve instruction? If so, what are some adjustments you have made? If not, where could you ask for feedback?
- How do students support one another in your classroom?

7

Conferring with Students During Class Time

Although it seems daunting to create time and space for conferring in the classroom, once you've established routines, it is essential for positive student growth. You will have to set up a classroom environment where students know how to self-select their learning, as they will need to be independent while you are working with them one-on-one. This chapter explores different ways to provide feedback to students in conferences during class time as they develop their portfolios.

Find ways to maximize your time with students when they are in your classroom. We need to let go of the idea that if we aren't lecturing students, we aren't going to make it through the content in time. Learning—*deep* learning—takes time. Too often, we spend our time following pacing guides without regard for how much learning students are actually doing. We focus too much on what we are teaching, then offer a single opportunity for students to demonstrate growth before we move on. This is not how most people learn. Conferring with students during class time can help to bring student voices into the formative process and can help us make essential shifts to our plans based on what we learn.

Small-Group Conferences Based on Need

There are several ways we can use small groups to confer with our students. Whether we are using intentionally grouped kids based on a formative assessment the day before or we have randomly placed students in groups for project work, we have opportunities to work with small groups for a variety of reasons. When we meet with small groups, we address one shared need of the group, whether we have formed the group with the intention of addressing a specific struggle or the group members, as they work, are asking for support on a given challenge. We acknowledge the challenge without stigmatizing it, and we have an opportunity to problem-solve and brainstorm as a group.

It is a good idea to use small-group conferences to build students' skills or extend learning among groups of the same level. You can also offer small-group conferences as a station in a class rotation where students can have questions on a particular skill or subject answered. Small-group conferences should be flexible enough to meet the needs of all the learners in the group and also allow ways for students to set goals and create action plans. To make these experiences meaningful and student-centered, ensure that each student has a plan and can speak to it when asked. Students' plans and goals can differ slightly based on their specific needs. Small-group conferences will also provide information for future planning and growth both for the students in each group and the class as a whole.

If direct instruction is called for during a small-group conference, make sure you tackle only one topic or skill at a time and provide a small "bite" of instruction with immediate practice before goals are written and plans are created. Students need to comprehend the challenge or area of stretch they will face before you set them on their way.

Individual Student Conferences

Emma Chiappetta calls the individual student conferencing process "clunky," and I agree. When I started working with students on this process, I wasted a lot of time, but I got a little better at it with each student. It was undeniable how useful the conferences were, so I wanted to implement them better and get more folks at my school to rally around them. Admittedly, when I started, I was spending too much time on the conferences, working hard to make them a part of my students' classroom routine. So, I started thinking about different ways I might save time.

The first thing I did was figure out a way to cut down on transition time between student conferences and also on the readiness of students when it was their time to go. As I mentioned earlier in this book, I used Google Forms to get students thinking about their learning portfolios before our conferences. This was a huge help. Usually, students got one class period to fill out the form. If they didn't complete it in that time, they had the remainder of the week to complete it, and conferences were then scheduled on a first-come, first-served basis. The quicker they could complete the form, the sooner we could chat. The forms gave me most of the data I needed; I was able to review them and write some clarifying questions so students could fill the gaps in what I read. This preparation ahead of time drastically cut down on the length of each meeting.

Next, I would put together a curated list of students—anywhere from 6 to 10 in a single period. I'd email this list to the class the night before and ask students to be aware of who came before and after them. I reminded them to have their evidence ready for our conversation and to be aware of the sanctity of the conferences. When it wasn't their turn, they were to be engaged in a self-selected activity taken from a menu. They shouldn't disrupt a conference except in the case of an emergency, and they should be ready to go at their assigned time.

On the day of the conferences, I made sure that learning targets, menu options, and the list of conferring students and alternates were all posted to the walls. After setting up the class and taking attendance, I would call the first name on the list. As the student approached me for the conference, they would erase their name from the posted list. In the 20 seconds of transition time between each conference, I had the opportunity to add a note or two into Google Forms. These notes helped me follow up later and served as a record of the gaps students shared with me in our conversations.

Ultimately, I found the more information I gave students ahead of time, the smoother the meetings went. Some students consented to be recorded, and when this happened, the class knew they needed to be thoughtful about the volume of their conversations.

Many people have asked me what students do while you aren't circulating. Routines and expectations play a big role: Since we had a classroom culture that valued this learning time, students treated one another the way they hoped to be treated when it came to be their turn to conference—and they knew they would all get their turn. Most of my classes were project-based, so there was always something a student could be working on, either in groups or independently, during conferences. In fact, students looked forward to the days when they could read, blog, or catch up on other writing activities.

Following Up on Student Conferences

The notes I took during conferences helped me determine how best to follow up with students and groups. I had access to all the action plans, which students regularly reflected on and worked through. During class time, if they had specific questions, I could circulate and capture them on "status of the class" spreadsheets.

In some of my classes, I could even empower a classroom manager to check in on student progress and maintain updates on individual plans. This was exceptionally useful in my journalism classes. We had a spreadsheet for student progress and deadlines that helped different newspaper staff communicate with each other; for example, if a news writer was almost done with their story, the spreadsheet would indicate that a photographer needed to get photos for that story and create a caption. This information was visible to all newspaper staff so that everyone knew whom to contact about what and whether stories and photos were ready for posting. This spreadsheet helped keep students accountable to one another and also freed me up to work with individual students who were having a hard time with the writing or research.

Whether in my English or journalism classes, following up on goals was essential. Doing so helped to plan my minilessons, influenced small-group instruction where appropriate, and clarified which students needed more support than I could give them during class time. If a student required additional support, I offered office hours before school, during free periods, and after school. Students also knew they could communicate with me directly via Google Docs or Voxer and we could discuss specific issues via electronic communication or make an appointment to talk in person.

 PERSPECTIVE: Dr. Jay C. Percell, Associate Professor, School of Teaching and Learning, Illinois State University

Over the years, I have attempted to hold conferences with students in several ways. The most productive iterations of student conferences occurred after I switched to an alternative no-points grading system. Certainly, this change was a complete paradigm shift and affected my instructional delivery, pace, timing, and assessments and the depth of student learning. In such an environment, introducing student-led conferences during class time was more feasible and effective than ever in my teaching career.

This shift changed everything about my teaching. First and foremost, it forced me to get a firm handle on backward planning (Wiggins & McTighe, 2005). Not only did I have to know the number of assignments and projects and amount of coursework necessary to achieve certain tiers, but I needed to articulate the skills and aptitudes I was looking for in student work. Individual assignments and projects were scored on a four-tier rubric, with the top two scores (Exceptional and Proficient) passing and the bottom two (Approaching and Far Below) not passing. I typically reserved Far Below for assignments that were never submitted and tagged those that still lacked a degree of proficiency as Approaching until they were of acceptable quality to pass. I allowed students three chances to revise any assignment or project. I was doing this work right around the time state content standards were being developed, so grading wasn't necessarily tied to standards like it is today. Rather, grades were based on assignment specifics and levels of academic quality I had predetermined and written into the rubrics, which is more akin to specifications-based grading modules, which are now beginning to gain prominence (Nilson, 2015).

In addition to affecting my planning, the new system forced me to tighten up the pace of my instruction. It allowed me the space to dive deeper into specific topics or themes that I chose or that my students were particularly interested in and to provide an overview of topics that may not have been as essential to students' overall learning. Not only did this give me the opportunity to establish the very structured weekly routine detailed below, but it also allowed space for regular student conferences to occur during class.

Once students recovered from the initial shock of a grades-free classroom, we settled into a very predictable and businesslike routine:

- Monday was usually devoted to the introduction of new concepts and the assignment of a new weekly writing assignment. Of course, if there were earlier concepts that needed some reteaching, those took priority over introducing anything new.
- Tuesday was an overflow day for reinforcing the new concepts introduced the day before.
- Wednesday was for journaling and freewriting.
- Thursday was for practice and skill work, usually surrounding some grammatical concept or literary device, using gradual release of responsibility.
- Friday was a conference/work day.

I realize that it is easy for "work days" to become little more than free time where students just socialize and procrastinate on their assignments. However, for whatever reason, possibly due to the system and structure I had in place, that is not how our conference/work days operated. Although the first few Fridays may have been dedicated to introducing the procedures and expectations, by three weeks into the semester, students already had a good amount of work coming down the pike. Whether they were revising a weekly writing assignment, completing a missed journal entry, getting a head start on a quarterly project, or simply working on the week's assignment, students were always busy and engaged throughout the classroom. These were some of my favorite days as a teacher. I would momentarily sit back and enjoy the buzz and hum of students working around the room.

Of course, Fridays were also when I would hold my student-led conferences. At certain points in the semester, usually near quarter or semester deadlines, I would assign each student specific days and times to conference. Other times, I might schedule a conference with a student over a particular issue I'd noticed in one of their assignments. Otherwise, these Fridays were open for students to either schedule a conference time with me or set up an impromptu conference if I had no standing appointment. Again, perhaps because of the routine and structure in place, or possibly because they mirrored real-world scheduled appointments, these conferences were rather productive. The expectation was that these conferences were strictly student-led; students were conferencing with me, not the other way around. At first, it may have taken students a while to realize they were meant to initiate the conference agenda (unless I had called the conference for a particular reason). However, once students warmed up to the concept, they began to view me as just another resource to help them make their work the best it could be. This outlook gave our Friday conferences a feeling of purpose and efficiency.

Student-led conferences gave me a positive sense of self-efficacy as a teacher, which was built primarily on the gains I saw among my students, who were able to prioritize elements of their learning, seek meaningful feedback they intended to use, and hone their skills through conferences and revisions to create high-quality versions of their work.

Prioritizing learning: The ability to prioritize workload is a real-world skill students need to learn, and conferencing in student-directed environments can help them develop it. My students had multiple assignments and projects coming at them throughout the week and had to determine which was most important at any given time. Learning to make wise choices about their work may even have been more important than some of the content they were required to learn.

Seeking meaningful feedback: How often do teachers spend hours poring over student work and providing ample written feedback, only to have students receive their returned work, glance at the score at the top, and ignore all the rest? By conducting student-led conferences during class time, we were able to mitigate this disheartening reality. Students led the conferences, asked questions, and sometimes even booked appointments.

The entire activity required students to seek only the information they needed and then work toward applying it in an authentic context. As a teacher who values feedback as the most critical element of the instructional process, seeing it connect in practice was incredibly rewarding for me while also being very beneficial for my students.

Honing skills through conferences and revisions: By receiving feedback and revising their work, students learned how to build upon and improve initial iterations of assignments. All too frequently, students can become solely wrapped up in completing their work as quickly as possible. During student-led conferences, feedback is communicated and received, and students can see how their revisions morph and change the quality of their work. They are no longer just working for completion but, rather, working to make sure their assignments are of the highest possible quality.

The only challenge I faced when implementing conferences was creating the conditions, environment, and expectations to make them run smoothly: shifting the grading paradigm, ensuring curriculum was skill-oriented, and being open to letting students lead conferences. Although this last point may seem intuitive, I found it quite challenging at times. Perhaps because we teachers spend so much time planning and preparing our lessons, our objectives, and the overall direction of our classes, we often have clear goals for students in place. Being open to switching those roles and allowing students to take the reins and set the direction of their learning is not always the most comfortable position for teachers. It took mindful intentionality for me to relegate my ideas to the sidelines. It took a concerted effort to minimize my voice, force students into the driver's seat, and allow them to pursue their interests. Even though it felt strange at first, I eventually became comfortable in my co-pilot role. Watching my students engage in their work, become more willing to take academic risks, and reap tangible benefits in their learning was incredibly rewarding.

Teaching is a labor of love. It is a professional vocation built on a desire to make a difference in the lives of others and to impact the community positively. Of course, every day is not sunshine and rainbows; teaching certainly comes with some inherent struggles. However, in my experience, the rewarding moments are enough to overshadow the challenges. And when I reflect on my time in the classroom, my most cherished memories are from those classes where we practiced student-led conferences. I vividly remember sitting at my desk between student conferences when I allowed myself to sit back and survey the scene. The room was alive with the soft buzz of busyness and productivity. Students were absorbed in their assignments, most working independently while others engaged in peer reflection. I remember thinking that this is what learning looks like, and I might only have had a chance to see it this clearly with the benefit of our student conference/work days.

Chapter Conclusions and Reflections

Successful student-led conferences take time. I cannot say this enough. Even though the tips I'm sharing with you throughout this book suggest a path, a culture needs to be developed to ensure the success of major shifts in routine. You need to have a portfolio system in place so students can draw from older learning and reflect on that learning. As they prepare for their in-class conferences, students can look for specific benchmarks and goals that they've co-constructed.

New routines will take time to take root in class. Time will be needed for practice and feedback. Remember that you and your students are learning together, and you will adjust the process based on the needs of your specific environment. You will always take notes, make revisions, and consider student voice in your planning before and after the conferences. You will learn more about what students know and can do from these conferences than from any assessment. If you allow students to share what they know and listen closely, you will be able to help them see their progress.

Remember also that these conferences are not meant to be assessed or graded; they are opportunities to advance learning through dialogue and feedback. If you need to keep track of the students with whom you've met, you can add a standards-aligned assignment that addresses their speaking and listening skills and provide relevant feedback there.

As you reflect on the content of this chapter, consider the following questions:

- What does your classroom routine currently look like?
- How are reflection and metacognition a part of the learning in your space?
- Do students have a choice over what and how they show what they know?
- Can your classroom run without you being in front of it? If not, what are some areas where you can release some control to students?
- What are your biggest concerns about implementing student-led conferences in your classroom?

Part 3

Student-Led Assessment Conferences (Gradual Release of Control)

So far in this book, you've read about the processes that need to be put in place to make student-led conferences using portfolios a reality. In this final section, we discuss how to use those processes to develop more robust, student-owned experiences using a gradual release of control. You will have the opportunity to explore what this looks like from the beginning of the year to the end and consider school-wide practices that assure student buy-in. You will also see how classroom practices can expand into parent-teacher conferences and practices that work for teacher evaluation and interview protocols.

Providing students with opportunities to develop the capacity to talk about and demonstrate learning in a meaningful way offers them a pathway to readiness outside school and empowers them to share their experiences as a way of better advocating for their futures.

As you read through this section, consider these questions:

- Who controls the learning in your space?
- How much time do you spend in front of your classroom?
- What structures do you have in place that empower students to take control of their learning?
- What visual reminders do you have around your space for students and families?
- What kinds of expectations do you have about learning at different points in the year?
- What are you most excited to learn about in this section?
- What are your goals for using what you learn in your current role?

8

First-Term Conferences and Expectations

Students who have not previously discussed their learning through conferences are bound to struggle with the process at first. They will require multiple opportunities to practice this process and feedback along the way to get better at it. The first conference of the year will be a testing ground for what works and what needs work. Give yourself and your students some grace and extra time to start mastering the expectations and objectives. Make sure to plan for extra time. This is not something you can do as an add-on; you must plan for it and stay the course until students grow more confident using the process.

In this chapter, we examine how to prepare students for this vital experience. We also explore how you can get ahead of the curve to create a positive learning experience you can share with students. Figure 8.1 shows a pacing calendar for building and setting protocols in your classes to help students prepare for defending their learning.

Preparing Students to Discuss and Defend Learning

The first conference students participate in will be clunky, especially if this practice is not widely used in your school. The quality of conversations will develop over time, as students become more adept at speaking about their learning. If you are starting from scratch, you will need some solid preparation.

Throughout this book, I have shared elements that need to be present to make the most out of these learning experiences. A culture of learning must be prioritized in class; making mistakes, setting goals, and celebrating growth should be embedded in the space.

Figure 8.1. Pacing Calendar for Creating Protocols

Month 1	Month 2	Month 3	End of First Term
Teacher introduces scaffolded reflection and portfolio process. Teacher provides feedback and models on reflection.	Students write reflections for most learning. Peers are included to provide feedback. Progress report is presented as the first formal one-on-one conference for goal setting.	Students track their goals with feedback from the teacher. Students prepare for first end-of-semester conference with a Google form.	First formal end-of-semester conference is held. Students co-construct success criteria with the support of a model video. Students prepare but with significant prompting. Goals are set.

At the beginning of the year, students will still be learning about the conference process, so meetings will take longer than they will later on. You will be doing a lot of the questioning, and students may not even know how to share their learning. Be ready for that.

Although forms are a great starting point for students that help scaffold the reflection process, filling out a form is different from having to sit and talk about learning. Reflection is not a natural, innate process for all learners, so you must ensure that you are modeling expectations from day one.

Think-alouds are invaluable when trying to help students understand metacognition and get them to go back to their "finished" learning and consider their processes. How did they manage to get from one piece of learning to the next? Where have they grown, and how do they know? You want to move kids away from reductive conversations about learning that focus on grades rather than actual learning. In the beginning, you will get a lot of that. This will be the most significant early hurdle.

It's important to scaffold the reflection process early in the year and model what good feedback looks and sounds like. When you ask students to write and reflect, you should write and reflect with them. Then, share what you have written with students and have them analyze how you showed your thinking and how you struggled and grew from the learning.

In the beginning, you will want to use a graphic organizer that asks students to pull elements of their learning that demonstrate specific standards or competencies using learning progressions. Another great strategy is to co-construct success criteria after watching videos of students talking about their learning. What do they notice? What do you think makes a quality conference? What do you hope to get out of students during your conversations? It's a good idea to hold quick goal-setting conferences with students before their first assessment conference.

PERSPECTIVE: Emma Chiappetta, Instructional Coach and Math Teacher (Part 3)

I use a five-minute goal-setting conference with students. These came about as the solution to a problem with self-pacing. When students control how much they work each day, they can take advantage of the flexibility and put in less than their best effort. At the same time, it might be true that a student is confused, didn't get much sleep last night, is struggling with mental health, or has a good reason for not mastering the content at the pace I expect. I put much trust in my students to make the right choices for themselves, and I have high expectations for them. Weekly goal-setting conferences help us find the right level to push them beyond their comfort zone while respecting their social and emotional needs.

I spread goal-setting conferences over the week, so I don't have to meet with too many students in a single day. I print out calendars with a box for each day our class meets. During the conference, we first talk about how things went with the goals from the previous week and then set goals for the upcoming week.

To set their goals, students take into consideration a variety of factors. They check a "learning menu" to see what they need to accomplish for the module they're working on in my class. They take stock of what they could get done in the previous week to make their goals more realistic. They ask questions such as these:

- What can I reasonably accomplish?
- What do I need to accomplish this week?

- What is going to get in my way?
- How did I do last week?
- How can I use that to set more realistic goals this week?

Most important, they consider their mental health and what may be happening in other classes. We have conversations about big summative assessments that may be going on in other classes that they need extra time to prepare for (or recover from), anticipated absences due to extracurricular activities, or other things going on outside the classroom that might create the conditions for a day when they just "can't do math."

Students are far more likely to achieve their own goals than arbitrary ones I set for them. Our conversations are realistic and prepare students to take responsibility for themselves and their mental health after they leave the classroom setting. Figure 8.2 is an example of a simple way to track goals throughout the week. You can create your own tracker with whatever information you want students to use to maintain and track their learning.

Figure 8.2. Weekly Goal-Setting and Tracking Calendar

Goal-Setting Conference

Monday	Tuesday	Wednesday	Thursday	Friday

Optimizing Quality Questioning to Get the Most Out of Conference Time

Now that you have students thinking about their learning in meaningful ways, you want to make sure that the questions you are asking are optimized for student growth and model the kinds of questions students should be asking themselves. These questions should not be leading or condescending but, rather, thoughtful and encouraging. It isn't uncommon at the beginning of the year for students not to know how to talk about their learning or how deeply they need to go. The questions you ask should help you glean the information you need to fully hear students' voices.

In her 2019 book *Hacking Questions,* Connie Hamilton cautions teachers not to supply answers to students' questions instead of letting them experience productive struggle. Instead, she suggests scaffolding your questioning in four parts: *question, prompt, cue,* and *reteach*. First, ask a question—for example, "How do you know you've met your learning objective?" If a student is stuck and looking for you to provide the answer, you prompt them, sending them back into their head to try to answer the question and reminding them of what they are answering—for example, "Remember when we learned about literary devices? Which one of the literary devices we discussed are you showing in your lit analysis paper?" Prompts give specific details that guide students toward the answer. Be patient and only offer a prompt if a student truly needs it. Wait time is essential, so don't rush the student's process. If the student still looks stuck after you have provided a prompt (or a few), provide a cue—what Hamilton calls a "visual, verbal, or kinesthetic signal that leads students to a successful response to the question" (p. 188). In my classroom, this cue was a poster I had on the wall that broke down reflection with a series of additional shorter questions that helped students refocus. Finally, you reteach, which offers an opportunity to use repetition and modeling to bring the initial learning back into focus only if the student needs it—in other words, only if the questioning, prompts, and cues haven't worked. In a conference, this might mean reteaching something that centers on the skill or content you are asking students to demonstrate in their portfolio.

Asking questions prior to the conference that are based on student responses to a preconference survey and goals and coming up with clarifying questions on the spot when students are speaking offer students multiple opportunities to go deeper during your conversations. How you model this practice early in the year will affect the degree to which students continue to question their own and one another's learning throughout the year.

Here is an example of a student response to the question "What feedback have you received recently?" on a preconference form: "I am mostly meeting standards in all my work; I noticed I'm better at certain things, such as essay writing, than at making a video deeply analyzing a character." If I saw this response on the spreadsheet prior to the conference, I would plan these follow-up questions:

- When you say you are "mostly meeting standards in all my work," what do you mean by "mostly," and what work in particular?
- You mention essay writing versus making videos. What do you find easier about writing essays? What is challenging about the videos?
- What might you do to go beyond meeting standards?
- What are your goals to keep improving?
- How can I support you as you seek to meet those goals?

The student may answer some of these questions while answering the initial question. I would need to actively listen and review any additional evidence provided at the conference, then ask on-the-fly clarifying questions to ensure the student had the best opportunity to show what they knew.

You can see an example of an early conference I had here: www.youtube.com /watch?v=c8MfsgjAnts&t=12s. This conference was more rehearsed than most, and it was during lunch, so there weren't any distractions. As you watch the video, notice who is talking and what you learn about the student.

Talking about learning is a risky business, but if we want students to really be in control of their narrative, we need to put that power in their hands and provide a safety net for the discussion. We must normalize this kind of nontraditional learning where students are in charge of what learning they demonstrate and how they demonstrate it and remove barriers to the natural vulnerability that comes when talking about teaching and learning.

Use Data to Shift Instruction for Personalized Learning

Student data shouldn't just end up on a spreadsheet or report card. Our obligation is to use the information we get from students to personalize the learning experience in a meaningful way for all kids. For the student in the example above, I would find a way to adjust the kind of assessments they were doing to have them show their best understanding. If they preferred to do that in writing, I would offer options that allowed them to demonstrate what they know and can do in that format.

As often as possible, I would allow students to create their assessments and the criteria by which they would be assessed. This became standard operating procedure in my mixed-media courses, where students went through the whole assessment design process themselves, carefully crafting the content they would work on and the product they would create. After making their decisions, they would create a rubric aligned with the appropriate objectives and a timeline for completion. I would confer with students and advise them on their choices, ensuring they selected topics and skills they needed to demonstrate mastery if they hadn't done so. Students were also expected to check in on goals and progress, and they worked independently on their projects.

PERSPECTIVE: Erin Quinn and Tara Vandertoorn, 8th Grade Humanities Teachers

Note: You can find Erin and Tara's work at www.creativitycollective.ca and www.r2b.ca.

In our 8th grade language arts classroom, our students have both literal and figurative room to breathe. In the approach that we have been developing over the past several years, our students design their projects within the language arts strands. They pair an "inhale"—text interpretation through reading, listening, or viewing—with an "exhale"—text creation through writing, speaking, or representing. Students choose texts to interpret on topics that interest them and that serve as a "just right" challenge for them. Students then create texts, thinking about an authentic audience that wants or needs the text they create. They then publish their work on our website, www.r2b.ca.

The assessment for this work occurs through conferencing. When proposing a new project, the student meets one-on-one with their teacher. They complete a project planning form, proposing what they will do. They also associate a goal with the work. We took the learner outcomes from our program of studies (that is, standards) and synthesized them into 16 distinct goals, 8 for inhales and 8 for exhales. The goals steer students toward specific skills and various kinds of texts. For example, "Explore the topic and theme in a text and explain how they interrelate" would lead students towards a fictional text, whereas "Research something you're interested in or care about" would lend itself to an informational text.

In the initial conference, the teacher and student discuss the project and ensure the student has all the tools and skills necessary to complete it successfully. We have developed graphic organizers and annotation bookmarks our students can use to organize their notes and annotations for their inhale work. In the conference, we also set a due date that is personalized to the student and reflects the project's complexity.

We meet formally with the student again on the project due date. At this conference, we discuss the student's work, the student talks about what they are proud of, we give lots of compliments and praise, and we discuss the next step in learning. Because the learning continues after the conference, the feedback is immediately applicable to the student's next project. The student also participates in the grading process. We have created a rubric that is general enough to accommodate many different types of texts, and we use the rubric to decide collaboratively on a grade for the work. Because students are a part of the grading process, they feel ownership and accountability for their work. In the final conference, we also review the student's planning sheet for their next project, approve it, and set a new deadline. Then, the work continues again.

Chapter Conclusions and Reflections

Once we've decided to shift the paradigm in our learning spaces, we must understand that getting students to the desired result requires us to scaffold the process. Not every student will be good at speaking about their learning immediately, but with the right coaching and support, they will all understand the power of the partnership you seek with them. Sometimes, your students will resent having to reflect and talk about their learning and may even beg you to "just tell them what to do," but I implore you not to quit on them. Telling them what to do is easy but will deteriorate the environment you seek to create. Stay the course, give and ask for feedback regularly, and continue to seek ways to improve the process in your learning spaces.

As you reflect on the content of this chapter, consider the following questions:

- What is your current process for preparing students to discuss their learning?
- If no process exists, where can you start tomorrow to give students this ownership?
- How do students set goals in your classroom?
- How do you use those goals to drive instruction?
- How are you collecting data to ensure that students are truly learning?
- In what ways can you include students in the assessment design process?
- How can you include student voice when creating or co-creating success criteria or rubrics?

9

Midyear Conferences and Growth

By this point in the process, you and your students have had some time to practice what learning conferences look and feel like. Some will see that they are a powerful tool that allows them to share their learning in a way that perhaps their daily classwork or projects have failed to do. Since we don't want to wait until the end of the year to see what kids have achieved, it is important to check in periodically and make adjustments. At this midway point, you and your students will begin to see the difference that portfolios and student-led conferences can make. You can use the chart in Figure 9.1 as a sample pacing guide for the middle of the year to ensure you are rolling out the necessary skills with practice in a timely fashion.

Use Portfolios to Help Students Identify Areas of Growth and Need

Earlier in this book, we discussed the systems and structures that need to be put in place for students to use the portfolio to see their growth and identify new goals based on needs. In the beginning, you likely prompted students to select portfolio items while teaching them to make good choices and then reflecting on those choices. By midyear, your students should have already gone through the collect, select, reflect, connect process a few times. At this point, you can continue to task them with reviewing their portfolio to set goals by identifying areas of growth and need.

Remember that you will want to co-construct success criteria with students and help them brainstorm different learning experiences they have participated in.

Figure 9.1. Pacing Calendar for Growing Student Agency			
Month 4	**Month 5**	**Month 6**	**Midyear**
On an ongoing basis, students track their own goals and set new ones when they are successful with teacher and/or peer support. Students continue to collect artifacts of learning.	Progress report conferences address current goals and progress. Students advocate for their own needs, asking for the feedback they require. Teacher asks fewer clarifying questions.	Students work with peers more for feedback. Teachers intervene when students express need or when need is evident.	Success criteria are modified with students if needed. Conferences are shorter as students know what to expect and what to prepare. Teachers use form responses to streamline conferences.

Adding these lists to the survey you share with them before conferences can help get them thinking about their progress without directly telling them what you know about them as learners.

Schedule days for students to review their work and track progress on their goals. Wherever possible, extend these responsibilities to students and create a protocol that they communicate to you. If you are using digital portfolios, students should share this protocol with you as soon as it's ready so you can provide feedback on it and update your online communication system (SIS, LMS, or other online communication tool) with the information for record-keeping purposes. Updating your portal with this information is another helpful way to keep parents or guardians in the loop.

Shift Questioning Power to Students

As previously discussed, teachers should develop a structure to model questioning for students. If you want them to be able to support themselves and one another, you must hand off the questioning power to them, allowing them to determine what is most important for their learning. Make sure to provide students with sentence starters to help them develop authentic questions aligned with the success criteria.

Ensure Students Are Meeting Goals

Clarity first, always. When a student sets a goal, it must be clear and measurable, and the action steps should have criteria attached to determine if they are successful. You will need to monitor student progress on goals so that you can intervene if necessary. When helping students develop the action plan, set a time for the first check-in and don't approach the student until that time comes. You are trying to build resilience and independence, and productive struggle is an essential part of doing so. It's OK if the student gets frustrated as long as they have a plan for moving out of that space. Be encouraging and supportive throughout the process. Remind your students of other goals they met and what that process looked like, and give them a chance to figure out the learning before you intervene. When students do require assistance, ensure that they reach out to peers before they reach out to you.

Use Data to Optimize Equitable Processes

Having students track their own learning and lead conferences about it is meant to ensure equity in the classroom. The more you get to know your kiddos, the more you can offer them exactly what they need to reach proficiency in their studies. You can ensure that all students succeed in this process by giving them a voice and an opportunity to feel proud of themselves as learners.

One way to make this magic happen is by tracking your own data and making choices based on what you learn from it. To ensure kids are getting the support they need, you want to give them multiple ways to show what they know. Do not make them feel stigmatized if they are moving slowly on their journey. Data can have an equalizing effect by taking us from a mindset of "I taught it so the students should know it" to one of "I taught it, now I need to see what they learned and make adjustments based on that." Too often, we are compelled to move more quickly than students learn because of a false need to cover all curricula. It doesn't matter if you cover it all if the students don't truly get it. So plan to check in more often than not and make decisions based on the reality of where students are and how best to keep moving them forward.

Deepen Student Reflection and Self-Assessment

Continued feedback is essential to making sure students continue to thoughtfully self-assess and reflect on their own growth, and there are various ways you can get them to go deeper in this work. Figures 9.2–9.5 show examples of midyear self-assessment inventories for you or your students to complete, either in notebooks or digitally. Be sure to also have students date their reflections as a part of the portfolio process in preparation for the conferences.

Students complete the Midterm Self-Assessment Inventory (Figure 9.2) in Week 6. I liked working with this sheet even though it required a lot of writing because it allowed me to express challenges I experienced throughout the learning process. It also gave me an opportunity to share how I addressed the challenges and how I improved from the practice.

The questions on the Midterm Self-Assessment (Figure 9.3) help teachers see the root problems students are facing and how well they think they are doing. In the portfolio handbook, though, you should show a student who is showing good progress in class, saying how they improved, instead of a failing student.

Students need to conference with subject-area teachers to assess strengths and weaknesses. They can use the form in Figure 9.4 (p. 110) to maintain a log of these conferences in the back of their writer's sourcebook. A writer's sourcebook is usually a notebook in which students keep track of classroom learning and minilessons. The teacher creates entries for a table of contents to be copied and tracked over time so that students can easily find learning. It is typical to also have a reader's sourcebook that functions the same way but is focused on reading skills. The log helps to ensure that students continually work on any areas that need improvement. You should keep such a log as well, as it will help with following threads in your class.

The sample conference notes chart in Figure 9.5 (p. 111) allows you to see what each student should be doing and the skills they have mastered. Consider adding a column where students can add their comments and reflections to what you've written.

Once students get into the habit of practicing conversations about goals and progress with both their peers and the teacher, they will learn to collect better data to show their learning. By midyear, this should become routine, with most students seeing the benefit of it. At this point, you no longer need to remind students to collect their learning or help them with their selection. Some students still may need scaffolds, but overall, they should be doing a much better job of organizing their learning and articulating where they have grown and what they still need support with. You are aiming for them to be self-sufficient by the end of the year—and I'm happy to report that, in my experience, they usually were.

Figure 9.2. Midterm Self-Assessment Inventory

Evidence (article, assignment)	Level of standards I am meeting overall	Successes: what I did well and how I was able to successfully do the assignment	Challenges: what I need some more practice with but have a basic under-standing of	Lost: what I don't know or understand; what I still need to learn or am missing in my work	How do I know this? Peer editing, teacher conferencing, or notes?	What I plan to do; goals set by myself or with Ms. Sackstein	What I have done and how it has helped

Figure 9.3. Midterm Self-Assessment

Class Expectations	Have Criteria Been Met?	Comments or Examples to Support My Assessment
Example: *I consistently did my homework and kept up with readings and assignments.*	Example: *Some of the criteria have been met. I don't think I'm proficient yet.*	Example: *I waited until the last minute to do all my* New York Times *reading, but I did get most of it done eventually. I could have managed my time better and disciplined myself to do an article every night.* *One thing I did well was some of the textbook readings. I found that when I did the reading the night before, the next day's class made a lot more sense. The reading that I was really prepared for was the article titled "Drugs." I was able to share my thoughts and questions in class the next day because I did the reading.*
I consistently did my homework and kept up with readings and assignments.		
I participated in class as much as possible, offering ideas and comments.		
I listened to my peers throughout class and understood that class discussion is one of the most effective means of learning.		

(continued)

Figure 9.3. Midterm Self-Assessment (Continued)

Class Expectations	Have Criteria Been Met?	Comments or Examples to Support My Assessment
I devoted a specific amount of time each night to read, reread, and reflect on what I read to better understand the text and be prepared to discuss it in class.		
I actively worked to improve my writing by revising constantly and having conferences when necessary.		
I independently wrote in my writer's sourcebook when ideas came to me or when I had reactions to texts I read.		
I kept both reader's and writer's sourcebooks up-to-date, making sure each entry was labeled in the table of contents.		
I reviewed the day's notes in the class blog every day to better understand the concepts.		
I wrote to get a point across while also engaging the reader, used organization skills, and learned writing strategies such as freewriting and brainstorming.		

Class Expectations	Have Criteria Been Met?	Comments or Examples to Support My Assessment
I engaged in public speaking, sharing ideas in both formal and informal presentations.		
I completed the map reading quiz and Early Americans test.		
I had to manage my time on several long-term projects such as the community map project and the world geography project.		

Overall grade I think I deserve for my mid-trimester progress report: _____

Overall grade I wish I earned for my mid-trimester progress report: _____

Overall grade I aim to earn for my first trimester report card: _____

Student Name: _____ Student Signature: _____

Guardian Name: _____ Guardian Signature: _____

Source: Copyright Starr Sackstein. Used with permission.

Figure 9.4. Conference Form for Subject-Area Teacher/Advisor

Name: _____   **Week:** 3 or 6 (circle one)

Date: _____   **Trimester:** 1 2 3 (circle one)

Working grade to date: _____ (on a scale of 1–4 based on the standards)

Standards being addressed at the current time:

Evidence of where student falls on the spectrum (projects/classwork/homework):

Plan for the next three weeks to establish opportunities to meet the standards (set goals to be re-addressed at the midterm point):

Source: Copyright Starr Sackstein. Used with permission.

Figure 9.5. Sample Conference Notes

Name	Standards Mastered	Standards That Need Work	Evidence	Goals
John	Creative writing, developing a narrative, formulating ideas, freewriting, speaking in class, using an organizational plan such as chronology	Dialogue grammar, group work, proofreading and revision, sentence structure, vocabulary	Participation in class discussion, skit on colonization, blog posts, explorer project, historical fiction short story, blog assignment	Improve proofreading and revision skills, dialogue grammar, sentence structure and vocabulary, and sophistication of writing
Pat	Brainstorming— sharing ideas, group work	Grammar, revision, speaking in class—verbal participation, time management	Skit on colonization, historical fiction short story, blog assignment	Improve revision skills—join the newspaper to help work on writing and grammar
Abby	Developing a narrative, note taking, proofreading, staying focused, using an organizational plan such as chronology	Geography, map skills, multistep directions, time management	Sourcebook notes—organized, community map project, historical fiction short story, blog assignment	More class participation, get work in on time; needs to continue to work on dialogue
Logan	Developing a narrative, geography, group work and dealing with other students in her group, reading comprehension (particularly poetry), speaking her mind, speaking in class, using an organizational plan such as chronology	Reflections, research, study habits, time management, works cited page	Participation in class discussion, sourcebook notes, world geography project, explorer project	Work on works cited page, show more depth in honest reflection; needs to continue to work on dialogue

(continued)

Figure 9.5. Sample Conference Notes (Continued)

Name	Standards Mastered	Standards That Need Work	Evidence	Goals
Juan	Finding evidence in the text, independent reading, social studies content, speaking in class	Freewriting, getting started on assignments, note taking, revision, speaking in class	Participation in class discussion, scrapbook project	Needs to work on staying on task and writing a full paragraph without so much support; verb tenses need work with being consistent; needs to learn what is important
Orit	Developing a narrative, freewriting, geography, group work, independent reading, literature circles, organization, research, using an organizational plan such as chronology	Getting started on writing assignments, map skills, proofreading and revision	Writer's sourcebook, skit on colonial times, scrapbook project, historical fiction short story, blog assignment, American Revolution essay	Needs to brainstorm before writing to develop better ideas and improve proofreading skills and punctuation
Lisa	No skills mastered	Note taking and organization, study skills	Historical fiction short story	Improve study skills, note taking, organization
Bart	Creative writing, developing a narrative, group work, independent reading, speaking in class, using an organizational plan such as chronology	Geography, map skills, online technology, revision, social studies content	Class participation, scrapbook project, explorer project, world geography project, historical fiction short story, blog assignment, American Revolution essay	Work on blog posting, revisions, group work, geography, and map skills

Name	Standards Mastered	Standards That Need Work	Evidence	Goals
Cyndy	Poetry, speaking in class, visualizing	Freewriting, organization, questioning, research	Class participation	Work on organizing their writing, staying on task, and becoming accountable for their work and progress
Lavell	Map skills	Getting started on assignments, writing and reading	Map quiz	Needs to stay in class for whole periods and use his energy to start working on his reading; needs to really engage in classwork and complete tasks
Al	Freewriting, map skills, social studies content	Handing in projects, note taking	Map quiz, blog assignment	Stay focused, take notes, do research, reflect—wants to sit by himself to help with his focus
Carlo	Developing a narrative, sharing ideas, using an organizational plan such as chronology	Vocabulary and word choice	Historical fiction short story, blog assignment	Work on building vocabulary
Dean	Developing a narrative, questioning, sharing ideas, using an organizational plan such as chronology	Sentence fluency, vocabulary and word choice	Historical fiction short story, blog assignment	Work on building vocabulary and improving sentence fluency

(continued)

Figure 9.5. Sample Conference Notes (Continued)

Name	Standards Mastered	Standards That Need Work	Evidence	Goals
Alicia	Creating skits, creating visual representations of work, drama (writing and presenting to the class), freewriting, reading comprehension	Following multi-step directions, meeting dead-lines, staying focused and on task	Scrapbook project, skit on the colony, historical fiction short story, blog assignment, American Revolution essay	Work on staying focused and on task, note taking
Zak	Developing a narrative, using an organizational plan such as chronology	Participating with peers in conversations	Blog assignment, historical fiction short story	Needs to make more effort to participate in class discussions
Jeb	Developing a narrative, formulating ideas, freewriting, map skills, questioning, reading comprehension, using an organizational plan such as chronology, varying sentence structure	Varying sentence structure, vocabulary and word choice	Historical fiction short story, blog assignment, American Revolution essay	Continue to work on varying sentence structure and learning vocabulary
Seth	Developing a narrative, following directions, map skills, note taking, organization, proofreading and revision, reading comprehension, technology, using an organizational plan such as chronology	Creative writing	Scrapbook, blog project, explorer project, Early Americans test, historical fiction short story, blog assignment, American Revolution essay	Participation, creative writing

Name	Standards Mastered	Standards That Need Work	Evidence	Goals
Sara	Developing a narrative, revision, using an organizational plan such as chronology	Proofreading	Historical fiction short story, blog assignment, American Revolution essay	Needs to continue to work on proofreading
Cyla	Developing a narrative, using an organizational plan such as chronology	Grammar, revision	Historical fiction short story, blog assignment, American Revolution essay	Continued work on revision, specifically dialogue and proofreading
Isla	Developing a narrative, using an organizational plan such as chronology	Adding details to a story, recognizing when she needs help, sentence structure	Historical fiction short story, blog assignment, American Revolution essay	Needs to start asking for help when she doesn't get something
Dom	Creative writing, developing a narrative, group work, literature circles—predictions, narrative writing, reading comprehension, social studies content, speaking in class, using an organizational plan such as chronology	"Do-now" responses, map skills, feature writing, note taking, organizational skills	Community map projects, explorer multi-genre project, scrapbook project, historical fiction short story, blog assignment, American Revolution essay	Improve sentence fluency, organization; work on book talk, writing piece

PERSPECTIVE: Emma Chiappetta, Instructional Coach and Math Teacher (Part 4)

Formative assessment conferences are valuable tools for completing long-term projects. A "project check-in" conference aims to

- Gain clarity on students' thought processes.
- Provide on-the-spot feedback.
- Redirect misconceptions and errors in thinking.
- Deliver individualized instruction specific to students' projects.
- Provide student-requested support.
- Inform future instruction and instructional strategies.

Having these kinds of informal check-ins with each student throughout a project ensures that they don't hit any roadblocks that might halt their progress and allows me to redirect them if they are headed on a dead-end path. These conferences also hold students accountable, because they need to show that they have made progress since the last conference and met the goals that they had set for themselves.

To prepare for these conferences, students fill out a form in Google Docs at least one day before the meeting (see Figure 9.6). The form asks them to summarize what they have been working on, their last goal, their next steps, and what support they need from me to move forward. The form is useful to them because it organizes their thoughts and embeds regular reflection into the project process. It's useful to me because it gives me a quick snapshot of where the student is and allows me to prepare to support them when we sit down for our conference. (In the case shown in Figure 9.6, I worked with the student to research different website-building software; we decided on Google Sites and began to build out the site together.)

Figure 9.6. Project Work Report Conference 3

Project Name: Style Markers   **Student Name:** Sam Wood
Date of Conference: 4/25/19

Since the last meeting, I had the following goals for my project:

Gather all of my data and start to have made some visuals.

Since the last meeting I accomplished . . .

I have started some visuals and I have all of my data.

My next steps are . . .

Finishing my visual representations of the data.

My most important concerns, problems, or questions are . . .

I want to enter everything onto a website/blog when I finish with everything but I am worried about how I am going to do that because I am not good at websites and that stuff. But I'm not too worried about it/ anything else.

Source: Courtesy of Emma Chiappetta. Used with permission.

Chapter Conclusions and Reflections

In this chapter, we explored how conferences can progress from the beginning of the year to the midway point, the growth you will undoubtedly encounter, and how to ramp up the process to put more control into the hands of the learner. We also talked about equity and how this process ensures that all students get what they need to succeed.

The midway point is often when we start to see progress, especially for students who have struggled for a long time. Once they succeed, they will feel less frustrated and more empowered to move forward. This is also when we may need to decide on instituting an intervention or adjusting the long-term goals. Having midyear progress conferences allows you to make the necessary revisions to ensure that no student falls through the cracks.

As you reflect on the content of this chapter, consider the following questions:

- Which students on your roster are currently struggling? How do you know? What have you done to support them? Are parents involved?
- Which students need enrichment or acceleration? How do you know? What have you done to support them? Are parents involved?
- Which topics seem particularly hard for your students to "get"? What have you tried to help them find success? How involved were you in that process?
- Is productive struggle modeled and supported in your class? What structures do you have in place to ensure that students know how to help themselves when they start to feel frustrated?
- What formative assessment processes do you have in place to ensure students aren't falling through the cracks? What is the protocol when a student needs additional help in this way?
- How are conferences improving in your space?
- Where do students still struggle, and how can you better support them?

10

End-of-Year Assessment Conferences

Many people argue that the best way for students to show yearlong learning is to engage in some sort of comprehensive final exam or project. Although these tools can help determine learning, they don't necessarily do the best job of allowing students to demonstrate their full range of growth. Creating an end-of-year assessment process that includes a portfolio of student-selected learning and an opportunity for students to explain their choices and answer questions about their growth can offer a more robust chance to do so. In this chapter, we explore an end-of-year (or -semester) conference and how it can be used to show growth over time and act as a summative learning experience. The pacing calendar in Figure 10.1 can guide you in rolling out your end-of-year conferences successfully.

Communicating Purpose and Providing Clarity

Whenever we move away from traditional practices in our classrooms, we must be transparent with students about what we are doing and why. Depending on what level you teach, some students may have already become accustomed to having learning "done to them." They aren't used to being part of the conversation, which means there will be pushback when you shift the dynamic.

By this point in the year, students should understand why they are having conferences and how best to communicate what they have learned. End-of-year conferences give students one last chance to show what they have learned over the year, so they are especially important for students who haven't managed to do so yet. Make sure to emphasize to students that you are on their side and want to see them succeed.

Figure 10.1. Pacing Calendar for Student-Led Conferences			
Month 7	**Month 8**	**Month 9**	**End of Year**
Students are in control of most aspects of the conference process. Expert groups are employed—shift with new peer experts to be able to function wilhoul leacher suggestions.	Google form is sent out for students to start reflecting on the full year of work. Students select their best work for their end-of-year portfolio and have identified goals that are still not met.	End-of-year prep begins; teacher provides an assignment sheet for preparation. Students are provided a choice of how to deliver their learning and given time in class to prepare in their chosen form.	Last conferences are initiated. Student presentations occur now for completion or graduation. Teacher is available for support when asked.

Since this is the final opportunity for students to demonstrate learning, you want to be clear about how they will be assessed and what they need to do to be successful. Make sure to reach out to parents of students who are on the borderline. As students prepare for their end-of-year demonstration of learning, have the success criteria you co-constructed visible for them to consult as needed.

Preparation and Use of Class Time for Success

In New York, the end of the year is late June. So, starting in late May, class time should be allotted for students to prepare their final portfolio presentations. The number of scaffolds you will have in place and the depth of knowledge you expect them to demonstrate should all be clear to your students at this point.

Figure 10.2 shows an assignment sheet I provided to my students to help them stay focused and show what they know in a variety of areas. The sheet includes links to the standards students had to meet; for younger students, you may consider a choice of student-friendly "I can" statements. The sheet also asks students to consider how they want to show what they know and provides them with various options for doing so.

Figure 10.2. Directions for Preparing for Final Self-Assessment

It is the end of the year, and now it's time to think about what you've learned. In preparation for your end-of-year self-assessment, I'd like you to prepare a bunch of materials. Because there are several options for how you can present your evidence of learning, read the general information and then the section that specifically refers to your delivery method.

General directions
You will prepare your evidence of learning to show what you have mastered, or at least become proficient in.

1. Review the specific standards for your class, as shown below.
   Standards for 11th Grade Newspaper
   > www.iste.org/standards/ISTE-standards/standards-for-students
   > www.corestandards.org/ELA-Literacy/W/11-12/
   > www.corestandards.org/ELA-Literacy/L/11-12/

   Standards for AP Literature and Composition
   > www.corestandards.org/ELA-Literacy/RL/11-12/
   > www.corestandards.org/ELA-Literacy/RI/11-12/
   > www.corestandards.org/ELA-Literacy/W/11-12/
   > www.corestandards.org/ELA-Literacy/SL/11-12/
   > www.corestandards.org/ELA-Literacy/L/11-12/
   > www.iste.org/standards/ISTE-standards/standardsforstudents

   Standards for 12th Grade Newspaper
   > www.iste.org/standards/ISTE-standards/standards-for-students
   > www.corestandards.org/ELA-Literacy/W/11-12/
   > www.corestandards.org/ELA-Literacy/L/11-12/

2. Review the work you completed this year and your reflections on it.
3. Determine which work shows your mastery of the standards.
4. You should be able to show your learning in each of the core learning groups with specific reference to the assignments:
   a. Reading
   b. Writing
   c. Speaking
   d. Listening
   e. Language
   f. Technology

(*continued*)

Figure 10.2. Directions for Preparing for Final Self-Assessment (Continued)

5. Make sure to indicate your areas of growth.
6. Did you meet your goals for the year?
7. What do you feel you could have done better? Why? How would you change this?
8. Make sure to grade yourself:

Explanation of grades

Grade	Level	Explanation
A	Mastery	Student makes inferences and applications that go beyond the simple and complex content that was explicitly taught. Student does the work consistently at this level without being told how to accomplish new tasks with associated skills.
B	Proficiency	Student demonstrates no major errors or omissions regarding any of the information or processes (simple or complex) that were explicitly taught.
C	Initial proficiency	Student demonstrates no major errors or omissions regarding the simpler information and processes *but* demonstrates major errors or omissions regarding the more complex information and processes.
P	Passing	With help, student demonstrates a partial knowledge of some of the simpler and some of the more complex information and processes.
ND/NI	Not demonstrated	Even with help, student demonstrates no understanding or skills.

A "+" indicates the student is approaching the next level of performance.

Source: From *Classroom Assessment and Grading That Work* (p. 58), by Robert J. Marzano, 2006, ASCD. Copyright 2004 by Marzano & Associates. Adapted with permission.

Written assessment

If you are writing your self-assessment, make sure to comprehensively discuss the standards for each of the core areas and the assignments/projects that address each of the sections. Make sure to write it like a reflection, using evidence from your work. Take screenshots to help show what you're talking about.

Multimedia assessment

If you use video, screencasting, or speaking (Voxer or voice message), I recommend you plan what you're going to say first.

In-person conference

If you are having a conference with me, you must come prepared with the above information and evidence. Think and prepare before you come for your scheduled appointment.

The conference schedule will be given out over the next week for each class. For those of you doing an alternative form of reflection, your work is due on _____.

If you have ideas about how to present the material, please don't hesitate to suggest them; no good idea will be turned down.

All prepared self-assessments are due on June 10th. All conferences will begin on June 1st, with the schedule to be determined.

After you have read these directions, please send me an email to let me know how you will do your end-of-year assessment so I can plan accordingly. I should receive your email **no later than May 19th.**

If you have questions, please email me or ask me in class.

Source: From *Assessing with Respect: Everyday Practices That Meet Students' Social and Emotional Needs* (pp. 122–124), by S. Sackstein, 2021, ASCD. Copyright 2021 by ASCD.

A week after sharing the assignment sheet, I sent out a separate form asking students to commit to a way of demonstrating their learning. This gave me time to prepare for students who chose in-person conferences. In my school, these conferences were separate from the schoolwide portfolio conference, which is presented to a committee. Seniors are looking at their body of work throughout their entire time at the school and sharing how their learning has made them uniquely ready for their chosen pathway after high school. Students not graduating but leveling up have to demonstrate their grade-level readiness for promotion.

You can see an example of an end-of-year student conference here: www.youtube
.com/watch?v=YgvFScT6vRc&t=10s. As you watch the video, take the time to notice
the student's vocabulary, growth, and process for demonstrating her learning. Her
preparation is clear, and the pride she shows in her work is rewarding. Consider
showing a video like this to your students as you discuss what exemplary work
looks like.

PERSPECTIVE: Lisa Hicknell, Consultant, Ontario, Canada

In Ontario, we are mandated to report grades twice a semester. Determining a grade was a collaborative effort shared between my students and
me. Prior to our grading conferences, students were invited to complete
a Google Docs form to identify what they perceived their achievement to
be concerning the course's overall expectations (summarized as essential
learnings in the form). Students used their Seesaw portfolios to review
their learning for each overall expectation, which made things super-easy
because all entries in Seesaw had been tagged. They then determined a
level of achievement based on the descriptive assessment criteria guidelines (inspired by Arthur Chiaravalli). They had to support their determi-
nation with evidence from their portfolio. Students were given time to do
this in class because I wanted to make sure they were able to be really
thoughtful about their responses. I appreciated having a window into what
the students were thinking about their achievements before sitting down
with them one-on-one.

I used the last few days of classes to sit down with students and discuss their achievement. We had their form responses and portfolios in
front of us. The students reviewed what they had shared in the form and
highlighted the evidence from their portfolio. I was able to ask clarification
questions as needed. After reviewing the levels of achievement they had
indicated for each essential learning, I asked the student what they felt

their overall grade in the course should be. Ninety-five percent of the time, what they indicated was what we went with. Sometimes they were harder on themselves than I would have been; other times I thought they were overestimating their achievement. However, in asking them *why* they had chosen their grade, they always revealed that my perceptions were only that—my perceptions. Students were the experts on their learning and understood it on a level that I could not notice from the outside.

One of the most powerful conversations I had during these conferences was with a student whom I perceived as not achieving his potential at mid-year. He had some great ideas when writing reflections about his learning, but they were mediocre when it came to producing products. He had identified his achievement significantly above what I had been thinking. In the conference, he told me, "Mrs. Hicknell, you like for us to work collaboratively when we're working on products, and you always group us randomly. I am an introvert and have typically been in groups with people who have much stronger and louder personalities. I try and offer my ideas and suggestions, but others overpower them in the group." He told me the ideas he had shared with the group and how they would have better met the expectations of the task. The conversation revealed a profound level of understanding that I would never have recognized had it not been for our conference. In the end, we went with the grade he had identified.

The conferences aren't only an opportunity for students to identify their grade; students also construct their own report card comments and evaluate their own learning skills, which are also included in the Ontario report card.

When I left my classroom role midyear, a parent shared this with me:

> I have been looking forward to seeing how the gradeless classroom would work this semester, and the new ways Laura would be challenged in her learning. I'm so impressed by your creativity and risk taking, and I feel grateful that you are stepping up to challenge the system on your students' behalf, so they can have every chance of success. I hope Laura has the privilege to have a teacher like you again one day.

Demonstrating a Full Year's Learning

I want to be clear that students need to demonstrate the requisite skills and content in order to be promoted. If you had a syllabus from day one that outlines what that learning was supposed to look like, students should have a strong idea as to whether they have met all the standards or competencies. If this wasn't expressly discussed, this is a good time to spend class time exploring portfolios of growth with exemplars for reflecting along the way. Learning that occurred earlier in the year can sometimes require some reminders if the course material doesn't naturally cycle.

This is also a great time to have students review class objectives. If holes exist in their performance, you can have them request remastery experiences to allow them to demonstrate proficiency before they present their final learning portfolio. One way to help them figure out where they stand is to create a survey after you have brainstormed as a class about all the meaningful learning experiences they have engaged in throughout the year. If your classroom is largely project-based, you will find that students are easily able to recall their experiences as they were personally invested in them. In addition, if you have students reflecting at the end of every learning experience, they have already taken the time to think about what and how they learned and how that learning met their goals and improved their overall experience in the class.

Practicing with Peers

Once students have selected how they will be sharing their learning, it is a good idea to have them practice their final presentation with their peers. Some students at younger ages may require a scaffolded script to help them hit all the notes. If your school has an advisory program, this could be the best place for students to prepare their scripts and presentation documents. Then they can practice with their peers in pairs, get feedback, make revisions, and practice some more.

If you don't have an advisory period, ask students to practice in class or have them record themselves, watch the video, and provide feedback. Once the video is made, the student should watch it with a critical friend and get feedback, then incorporate that feedback in further practice. Then the teacher can provide support. Presenting becomes a different genre when it isn't a conversation but a presentation with defense, with the student standing at the front of a room before peers and adults, the focus of everyone's attention. A key aspect are the questions and responses that come after the student communicates the key takeaways. Students will feel more confident provided they have had ample opportunity to say what they need to and be challenged with questions about their presentation. Practice is good for the presenter as well as the questioner, and the two can even switch roles. This is especially helpful if students will need to speak in front of a panel or small group later as well.

Exit Portfolio Conferences and Presentations for Graduation or Grade Promotion

In lieu of a final exam, you can offer students a more meaningful learning experience where they explore their growth, discuss their progress, and connect their learning across disciplines as they prepare to move on after graduation or into the next grade. In our school, students were expected to present for individual classes like mine and then to give a final presentation to a larger committee or panel. Seniors had to create a presentation that showed their progress over the last four to six years (depending on whether they were with us for middle school, too). In these presentations, students aligned their learning to their intended fields of study in college, thinking about their readiness and preparation. (See Appendix F on page 175 for an example of a script that a former student of mine used to reflect on her four years in high school during an end-of-year presentation.)

I loved being a part of the panels that listened to these presentations, which usually comprised teachers, administrators, parents, and other students. The students were to assess the presentation with a rubric and provide feedback to their peers after engaging in a Q&A about any areas that the presenter didn't directly address. Typically, the entire senior class was assigned to be on a panel, with time slots set up by our programmer and given to students at least two weeks in advance. In lieu of final exams, students were scheduled into sessions that usually lasted two hours. In each room, there were about four or five students and at least two teachers and an administrator. Parents were invited, and students could invite additional folks, too. Classes were not in session at this time, so students only came in for their window of time to present and watch the other students who were in their group. It was truly amazing to bear witness to this much learning.

If you want to set up these kinds of presentations in your classroom, you can generally assume that three or four students could present per 45-minute class. Draw up a roster with the order of presentations and co-design rubrics with students, who should also determine protocols and expectations for speakers and listeners. Consider also making feedback forms that students can use to address questions or comments to presenters.

Chapter Conclusions and Reflections

In this chapter, we reviewed how to ready students for end-of-year conferences and presentations using a full year's worth of portfolio learning. We discussed what classes could look like and how to bring students' learning experiences together. Students have the capacity to really explore their own learning, talk about their growth, and speak to how it all connects.

As you reflect on the content of this chapter, consider the following questions:

- How do you currently assess a full year's worth of learning?
- Does your method include students in the process?
- If you are still using a final exam, what other components can you add to ensure equity and voice for each student?
- What structures are in place for students to reflect on their learning at this time? Is there a way to make them public if they aren't already? Where might you start?
- What exemplars do you have that you can share with students as you push forward with this paradigm?
- What are your fears or concerns about using this kind of method to determine student proficiency in classroom learning?
- Where might you need additional support to better ready students for these in-depth conversations and presentations?
- Do you have a committee at your school that handles grading and assessment? Can you raise interest to move to a system like this?

11

Using Student-Led Portfolio Conferences Instead of Parent-Teacher Conferences

It has always surprised me as a parent that my child wasn't expected to participate in parent-teacher conferences. I distinctly remember one time, when my son was in elementary school, sitting at a little table in the back of the classroom. The teacher had my son's work and her gradebook open in front of her, and she proceeded to tell us what we already knew because we had access to the school's online communication tool. It baffled me that my son, who was seated outside the classroom door, wasn't allowed to hear what was being said about him and his learning. Why are we afraid to let students participate in this conversation?

As a teacher, I have always wanted my students present for these discussions, especially at the secondary level. It is important for parents to hear from their children about their learning; teachers are not the only ones who should be able to speak to it. Parent-teacher conferences are in need of a major makeover. In this chapter, you will learn how you can include students in these discussions and use these communication opportunities as a way to really show learning as it is happening instead of just talking data from the gradebook.

Shifting an Antiquated Tradition

Parent-teacher conferences usually occur twice a year. I remember when my parents stopped going to mine and shifted all their energy to my brother, since I didn't seem to need the check-in. The perception was that if a student was doing well, there was no reason to check in on them; parents with multiple kids should put their energy where it seems most useful.

As a mostly 12th grade English teacher of AP or journalism students, I got quite used to not seeing very many parents show up on back-to-school nights or parent-teacher conferences—that is, until my school did it differently. We were a portfolio school and had an advisory system in place, so students were already expected to be a part of the experience. In most schools, when parents are present alongside students, you get a three- to five-minute time slot to share your gradebook, mention what is missing, and give any high-level information you haven't communicated in a phone call earlier. It often feels redundant.

Of course, the way schools work now, most of the grade information is available 24/7 via online gradebooks, so parents don't need teachers to tell them what is missing. What they really want to know now is how they can help. Is there anything that isn't communicated regularly they need to know about? We no longer need a special night twice a year to communicate with parents. It might be more useful to hold multiple smaller events throughout a term where parents, teachers, and students can share ideas about progress with evidence and kids drive the conversation.

As you read on, ask yourself these questions:

- How does my school do parent-teacher conferences?
- Are students involved?
- What is the turnout like? Why?
- How can we improve that communication?

Including Students in the Communication Process

How do you make time in class for students to prepare for conversations about learning when you already have more content to teach than time to teach it? The answer is that sometimes you need to make tradeoffs for the betterment of students' learning. You need to periodically stop and allow students the time to reflect on their learning, collect their thoughts, and practice talking about what is going well and why.

You'd be surprised how seriously students take this process. They know how important it is to be doing the learning and to be able to understand what they are learning and why. Having the opportunity to go through their portfolios, select evidence to share, and talk about how they are meeting targets in a meaningful way also gives them the chance to proudly share their progress and how they are setting and meeting goals.

What if students had time in class to do this? Time to script what they want to say and time to practice so that when they come in with their parents, they are well prepared to discuss their learning experience. As a matter of fact, if this became the norm, parent-teacher conferences would be rendered little more than ceremonial, because kids could have robust conversations with parents at home about their learning. No more frustrating answers to the question "What did you do at school today?" or "What did you learn at school today?" I can't tell you how many times my son has told me he learned nothing at school that day. If he had a test, I might hear an "I think I did OK on my math test" or "I bombed my Chinese test." When I remind him that I'm not really interested in that part and that I'm eager to hear what topics he is learning about and what he thinks about them, he sometimes offers a bit more, but not without my prying questions. We need to change that dynamic.

Empowering Students to Lead the Conversation About Their Learning

Including students in these conversations starts with giving them the vocabulary to talk about what they are learning. Then, we must encourage them to use that vocabulary to self-advocate or follow up on their learning in class. We need to create structures in class that allow students time to reflect on their learning and to talk about their goals, not just with the teacher, but with a wider audience.

An advisory period is a perfect time to do this work. Since my advisory students weren't necessarily in my English or journalism classes, I knew them on a different level. We had shared time that was meant for relationship building, not just academics, and as an advisor, I was there as an advocate, not just as an evaluator. They had access to their portfolios, and so did I. They spent time in advisory working with partners to select the best evidence of their learning and they had time to question one another before having to have those conversations with the adults in their lives.

How Does a School Make This Shift?

Once you have decided as a community that you no longer want students to be left out of conversations about their learning, you will need to communicate the shift to parents. This is not going to be comfortable for everyone, so explicitly explaining the "why" of the shift is essential for folks to be on board. Since parent-teacher conference dates are usually built into the calendar, consider sending out invitations for guardians to sign up for time slots that specify they should bring their child(ren) in with them. Setting up appointments is easier for elementary teachers, who have a single class. Secondary teachers are encouraged to use an advisory structure to help one teacher become an advocate for students and also help facilitate the conferences without an overt academic knowledge of every student. For example, in my advisory, I would be in touch with my advisees' teachers, so I had some information and could help advocate for them. And when it came time for conferences, I was reaching out to my 20 students and their families to schedule them. We would make appointments so we knew who was coming and when. Each appointment was set up for 15 minutes, and parents were discouraged from seeing the other teachers while they were there. If they had an interest in meeting with faculty, there were sign-up sheets for setting appointments. Students were encouraged to be a part of those conversations with teachers, too. In my room, I had several stations set up with computers where students and their guardians could sit and have conversations about learning. If parents wanted to speak with classroom teachers, they could sign up for a separate meeting, but these nights were not meant to address issues with teachers.

In my high school classes, students were already practicing reflecting on their learning and talking about their progress both in our one-on-one conferences and with their peers. Some of my 9th grade students may have needed a script to get going, but for my 12th graders, talking about learning was second nature.

During class time, using the co-constructed criteria for what goes into the portfolio, students should review their reflections and make choices about what they want to share with their guardians. You should circulate while students are working in groups reviewing criteria. Some students will want to work alone in the beginning, but be prepared to help students get ready for their conferences using the four-step collect, select, reflect, connect process, which allows students to review their body of work and decide what best shows what they know and can do. A review of this process follows.

    Collect: As students are learning, they need to keep a collection of their completed work, whether in a physical folder or on a digital platform like Google Drive.

    Select: Students go through their collection and select the work that they believe shows their best learning or the most progress. You can help students by giving them a checklist of criteria to determine what makes work worthy of selection for the portfolio. This list can be normed by vertical teams or by grade-level teams, depending on students' age and the school environment, but ultimately, students should be the ones to select the pieces for inclusion.

Reflect: You should determine both when students reflect and which mode of reflection will best demonstrate their understanding. My students reflect on all their major assignments as part of the process. When it comes time for them to present, they have an easier time because they have already done so much preparation through their prior reflection. The depth of students' reflection will likely vary depending on their age, maturity, and comfort level with the standards and content.

Connect: Portfolio time is a great opportunity for students to explore connections and show mastery of skills and knowledge across content areas. The connect step also allows for further practice in different settings.

Once students have put their portfolios together, it's a good idea to get them practicing how they will actually present their learning. Pairing students up in advisory periods or another agreed-upon period of the day allows them the time to work through a script (if one is provided for scaffolding purposes) or to write a script or an outline of their own that will increase the coherence of their presentation. This is the moment when students can really articulate what they know and can do and where they need to continue to work for greater depth of learning. Because students have prepared and we can be certain that they are able to talk about their learning, teachers are taught not to get involved in the conference between students and their guardians but, rather, to facilitate from the side with technology or help present physical collections of student learning.

 PERSPECTIVE: Layton McCann, 5th Grade Educator, Falls Church City Public Schools, Virginia

Note: Layton has been teaching since 2005 and is a National Board–Certified Teacher.

In 5th grade at Oak Street Elementary, we believe that student reflection and goal setting are a vital part of the learning process. Guided by their teachers, students spend time at the end of the first quarter reflecting on their successes so far in the school year, as well as on areas in which they want to grow and improve. We are an International Baccalaureate Primary Years Programme school, so students know that *how they learn* is as important as *what they learn*. The verbiage on our reflection template (see Appendix C, p. 156) matches what's on the schoolwide report card. We spend time with students working through what all the words mean and how the text applies to the expectations in the classroom. It's important that we are transparent about the feedback they will receive on the formal report card. They become familiar with it, and it's viewed as a team effort.

Next, students set achievable goals for themselves in all academic areas as well as for their work habits and behavior. Students have the opportunity to share their thoughts with teachers and classmates to brainstorm ideas.

Students then think about what they want to share with their parents and teacher during their upcoming student-led conference. We provide a suggested template that they use to script what they want to say (see Appendix D, p. 166). They choose artifacts of work they are proud of and share what it shows about them as learners. They choose which successes to discuss and which areas for improvement they want to focus on. Some students choose to create a slideshow to accompany what they share, especially if their artifacts are digital.

During the conference, students take their leadership role seriously and share openly and honestly with their teachers and parents. We have found that students' assessments of themselves are accurate and more meaningful since they come from the students themselves. The teacher is ready and willing to support the student as they share, as well as to add their own perspective, especially if the student is being too hard on themselves. The teacher also takes notes during the conference and makes copies for the student and their family.

Teachers and students revisit the goals at the end of the second quarter. Students reflect and adjust for the rest of the year. While the school does not set aside time in the spring for conferences, parents may request a conference at any time to check in on student progress. We value the reflection process at Oak Street and weave it into most assignments and certainly all projects. During our four-month-long capstone project, called "Exhibition," students add weekly reflections to a journal on their progress, contributions to the group, and what they are learning about themselves as learners.

 PERSPECTIVE: Meredith Klein, Middle School International Language and Literature Teacher

What is the purpose of conferences? Most schools view them as a time for teachers to meet with the students' families and discuss each learner's progress reports and grades. Rather than maintaining a teacher-centered approach, schools have an opportunity to reimagine how conferences can be student-led. Educators should guide students to be able to lead their own conferences and demonstrate their own learning in ways that are meaningful and relevant to them. As a result, students internalize the value of a growth mindset, families are able to better appreciate their students' unique and relevant learning, and educators are able to assume more of a coach or facilitator role that places the student at the center.

I saw the benefits of this approach firsthand when, at one previous school, all student advisors came together to revise our process for our middle school students. Guided by the expertise of the learning support lead teacher and the counselor, all advisors used a framework that had students planning their own conferences during their advisory time. In this model, the advisor is a student advocate and not responsible for a specific course or grade. There is a relationship and level of trust between advisor and student that serves as a strong foundation for the student to develop their confidence and to present themselves holistically as a learner. Students use a template to streamline the collection and organization of their learning evidence by following these steps:

- Reflect on their learning to date in each class and record their ideas on their planning document.
- Identify common themes and connections in any reporting comments.
- Identify what has been most meaningful for them in each class. This could be based on interest, a challenge to work through, or anything else that gives them a sense of accomplishment.
- Select a range of examples of learning that they think best demonstrated their growth. This could include learning activities, assessments, projects, or unit reflections.
- Consider including an example of a struggle or conflict and a self-assessment of how they dealt with that challenge.
- Articulate in their own words what they learned from these experiences, including content, skills, and larger concepts.
- Identify specific competencies that they feel they have improved upon and articulate a non-numeric academic grade that is linked to subject-area content and skills.
- Discuss what goals they should set to keep their learning and inquiry going.

There are several benefits to coaching students to lead their own conferences. For one, students are literally at the center of the discussion around their learning and progress. This provides an opportunity to balance qualitative data over just quantitative data. Put another way, students are the subject of the learning, so they should be the ones who share how it has affected them personally. Additionally, since students are unique learners with their own identities, backgrounds, learning styles, strengths, and goals, shifting the focus to their perspective builds upon the principle that learning is personal. Further, student-led conferences create an opportunity for students to develop self-advocacy skills; students are not passive listeners of adults talking about them, but rather are driving the conversation around their learning successes and needs.

As you consider how a similar framework might work in your school, there is one simple change that you can make: write comments directly to the students. Rather than report about them in the third person to other adults, treat comments as an extension of the conversations you would have with students personally. This simple adjustment can help your school to refocus the design and purpose of comments and conferences; both these practices are reflections of how well educators know, see, and support students, so that all learners feel valued and capable of advocating for themselves because they have the information they need to set goals and ask for help.

There are many varieties of student-led frameworks that can be adapted to reflect the context and culture of each school, but the underlying hope is that all schools view this approach as one that raises the prominence of students' voice. And by advocating for student-led conferences, schools send the message that their voice not only counts but is, in fact, the most important one. Student-led conferences reflect a culturally responsive approach that celebrates the connection among identity, experience, and learning style. They invite students to share and show what they have learned and what is meaningful to them. Most important, they encourage students to be in partnership with adults and to use their support and guidance to take ownership of their learning.

By guiding students to know who they are, how they learn, and what they are passionate about, we can reimagine the purpose of conferences to be opportunities for advocacy and agency. As schools continue to adapt to the myriad of changes that influence what "education" means, one constant mission will remain the same: students finding their purpose and deciding how they want to contribute to the world around them. Student-led conferences are one important step toward making this vision reality.

**PERSPECTIVE: Lance Piantaggini,
High School Latin Teacher**

Providing more consistent feedback and having students choose their own learning evidence in 2022 serendipitously coincided with our first whole-school student-led conferences (SLCs), which replaced traditional parent-teacher ones with historically low attendance. The new format resulted in about 98 percent family participation. For the SLCs, each student chose a 20-minute time slot to share three pieces of evidence with someone from home: something that they were proud of, something that was challenging, and something they wanted to do better on. Teachers oversaw a cohort of about 13 students who had a few short advisory periods to collect the three pieces of evidence and plan out a brief presentation (e.g., "Grandma, I chose this because . . ."). On the day of the conferences, the teacher was present in the room while the students presented to someone from home. All the work was student-led.

The SLCs were a small-scale version of the portfolio system in place for my Latin classes. My mostly 9th grade students were uploading learning evidence from class—usually pictures of their notebooks—about once every week to Google Classroom. Practically speaking, we set aside 10–15 minutes in class for students to get out their laptops or phones to gather this learning evidence. We did a lot of modeling, showing students exactly where to click on Google Classroom. We also projected criteria that were crucial because they provided a rationale for how the learning evidence showed students' understanding of Latin. This is when I really had to begin flexing my feedback muscles. In fact, I had not really had much experience with feedback in my nine years of teaching. I was prepared with a plan, but carrying out that plan was no simple task. I quickly learned that when you ask for student voice, you really do get it. At this point, I also acknowledged that what I had always thought of as self-assessment was, in fact, only self-grading; that is, I had not been asking students to justify the grade they chose. Selecting a grade is nowhere near as meaningful as providing a rationale for doing so.

Here is an example of a student's rationale for their self-assessment:

I have been following on about the "crazy for carrots" story, doing the illustrations on it and *ursus Avaro*. I have been listening but comprehending the Latin I have read and understanding how the Latin is said. I have been responding by engaging in discussions of the stories we have made. I have been showing my understanding by translating the *ursus Avarus* text, and I have been asking as many questions as possible when I couldn't understand the Latin.

Students used class time to upload their learning evidence. This is what Sarah Zerwin, in *Point-less: An English Teacher's Guide to More Meaningful Grading* (2020), would call "protecting" that time. As we monitored and modeled, we could catch some learners struggling to provide rationales in real time and ask them to explain more, or to describe why they chose their evidence and how it showed their learning.

In this new feedback phase of mine, I found that some students were very articulate in expressing how their chosen learning evidence showed their understanding of Latin as a result of the *process* criteria, while others struggled to connect those dots. I was fortunate enough to be in a building with a writing specialist, so I asked him to come in and give a few short lessons on writing these rationales. In full transparency, this was entirely off-brand for me as someone who maximizes the amount of Latin in class. Devoting precious class time for something in (gasp!) English was exactly what I avoided. Yet the benefit was undeniable. Whatever minutes of Latin I gave up for that focus on writing were made up for when it came time to respond to rationales throughout the quarter.

Chapter Conclusions and Reflections

In this chapter, we discussed the challenges inherent in antiquated parent-teacher conferences. So much has changed over the last decade in how we communicate with families that it feels silly to hold on to strategies from the past just because we are afraid to try something new. What if we recorded conversations with students about their learning and shared the recordings with parents, or had students present to their parents via Zoom during the school day for a few minutes, thus reducing how often they actually have to come to the building? What if we tried something different to engage parents and, when challenges arose, didn't wait until a specific day to reach out to them?

Parents want to be informed about what is happening at school, but they are busy, too. We need to find ways to have two-way communication that allows students to be a part of the process. What would that look like for you and students in your school?

As you reflect on the content of this chapter, consider the following questions:

- What could you do tomorrow to start shifting the conversation to student-led conferences even if your entire school isn't on board?
- How could you engage parents in a meaningful way and maintain open lines of communication?
- What kinds of reflection can you do as a teacher to make time in your classroom for students to own this conversation? What could they replace?
- What would be the greatest challenges in making this shift?

12

Teacher Portfolios to Highlight Professional Growth for Tenure and Beyond

In this book, I have discussed the need to provide models to ensure student success in learning. One way you can demonstrate how to create and maintain a portfolio is to keep an up-to-date professional portfolio that shows your own growth over time and achievements from your career. When I sought tenure for the first time what feels like a million years ago, I was required to submit a binder that spoke to my experience as an educator and showed why I was worthy of tenure. This was very similar to the portfolio I had to create when completing National Board Certification. The binder was divided into the following sections, with reflections affixed to each included piece of evidence:

- Observations and commendations to show growth over time
- Parent and community outreach
- Evidence of professional learning and commitment to career development
- Student work samples
- My best lesson plans and projects or assignments
- Things I was proud of, such as letters from students and parents or colleagues

This binder housed some of my earliest writing, certifications, and memories from my early days in the classroom. I actually schlepped this thing around with me when I was interviewing for my second and third positions. It wasn't until I had migrated my portfolio to a digital version at my third school that I joined a portfolio committee. We were looking to provide a model for students as they built websites with their evidence of learning over time, so I shared mine, which you can see here: https://sites.google.com/a/wjps.org/sackstein/Home.

If we go through this process ourselves, then we can better understand the challenges students may encounter when they are selecting their artifacts and working to tell their own story. It is always best practice to complete the assignments, assessments, and portfolios we are asking kids to complete so that we can truly understand how clear we are being and can make adjustments before the students encounter any hiccups.

I have spent the last 20 years collecting evidence of my professional impact and growth. Today, my "portfolios" include the professional publications I've authored as well as my website, MsSackstein.com. Whether it is the blog posts that honestly document my successes and challenges, the books, my social media feeds, and testimonials from students and teachers about the work I've done with them, or a collection of personal experiences and teacher work that demonstrates how my coaching has developed their understanding—all of these "count" as models of my success. My class websites also document my learning growth along with that of my students. (You can see two examples of those sites at https://sites.google .com/a/wjps.org/apliterature-wjps/home and https://sites.google.com/a/wjps.org /the-blazer---newspaper-class.) My students used these sites to find clarity, access exemplars and resources, and make them more independent as learners.

Since the world is largely digital now, we have to be aware of the footprints we are creating and the story they tell. Whether we like it or not, everything we do is being documented, and this documentation is especially comprehensive for students who have lived their entire lives online. As we curate the story, we need to be intentional about what we post and when. This offers teachers another opportunity to model for students the impact of their choices in the digital space.

Since we need to model the practices that we want students to use, I encourage you to take the time to create your professional portfolio. Even if you have tenure and aren't required to do so, I still encourage you to work through the exercise. Any interviews you have after you work through your portfolio will serve as your version of a student-led conference. I even recommend you record yourself talking about the portfolio, either as a screencast or as a video in which you capture your learning while sharing your artifacts.

Here is one way you might consider organizing your portfolio, but remember that there is no single "right" way to do it:

- Evidence that supports areas in your career you are proud of
  —Observations
  —Letters of commendation
  —Awards you have won
  —Achievements
  —Field trips
- Evidence of growth over time
  —Revisions of projects
  —Student learning
  —Professional learning you've done (credits or transcripts)
- Evidence of leadership and school involvement and growth
  —Committee involvement and growth
  —New classes or courses, clubs you created for your schools
  —Instructional coaching
  —Mentoring
- Evidence of commitment to the profession outside your classroom role
  —National or regional organizations you are a part of
  —Conference presentations
  —Speaking engagements
  —Publications
- Parent and community outreach
  —Communication logs
  —Parent letters
  —Community organizations and relationships

For each piece of evidence you select, make sure you reflect on why you chose it and what it represents. How does this tell the story of you and your career? How do you want to document your impact? Perhaps you leave space for the goals you are setting now and add evidence at each new milestone.

It is easier to collect artifacts when you know what you are working toward, so make an objective or impact statement and then outline areas that make sense for your career path. I would love to know what this experience is like for you and would be interested to see what you come up with. Do not hesitate to reach out and share links to your digital work.

Final Thoughts and Next Steps

As you consider the many ways to empower students in the learning process, you must always go back to a basic understanding of the relationships you've developed throughout the year. Learning is a complex and messy process, and for far too long, many of us have treated teaching like a one-size-fits-all undertaking where we fill our empty students with knowledge and skills. To fully assess the nuances of individual students, we must adjust how we see them and give them a voice in the assessment process.

As your students begin to collect evidence in their portfolios, you will need to find a system that works for your school or district, create a protocol for how long you will keep student portfolios, and decide whether you'd like to release students' work once they graduate. What will that process look like? How can students get a downloadable version of all their work? (Hard copy is easier to figure out, as they can literally take it with them.)

How would you like to use these portfolios with students who are still in the district? Who will have access to them—current teachers, new teachers, guidance counselors? Is it up to the students? Who owns the data? Your system is going to need to figure these things out.

If this is not your first time implementing student-led conferences and engaging students more in the formative assessment process, consider how to level up these experiences. How might you increase the level of rigor around these conversations? How can you include students earlier in the process? Can you get them to participate in the curriculum and assessment design process? What would that look like? Just imagine what that kind of involvement could lead to: faster intervention times, more student engagement in the IEP process and goal setting, and students being able to articulate why they want to take classes and why they belong in those spaces. It can fundamentally change the way you think about scheduling and promote accountability and buy-in for more students.

If these are things you and other folks in your building are interested in exploring more closely, I recommend putting together a committee that can assess where the school is right now, conduct a needs assessment (see Appendix E on page 170 for an example), and create a plan for moving forward. In addition, it makes sense to create a pilot group, as shown in Katie Harrison's Perspective section in Chapter 4 (p. 53). The more people you can get involved in the planning process, the more likely it is that you will get full adoption when the time comes. A pilot group can also create a portfolio handbook that is unique for your school setting and answers all the questions teachers, students, and families may have. Figure 12.1 shows an example of the

---

Figure 12.1. Sample Portfolio Handbook Table of Contents

I. Definition
   1. Portfolio planning
   2. Kinds of portfolios
       i. Work in progress
       ii. Year-end presentation
   3. E-portfolio
   4. Exemplar
   5. Variations: differentiated for the individual student according to grade and level
   6. Calendar for the year: trimester breakdown of portfolio expectations in the class
II. General
   1. Self-assessment
   2. Timetable: high school and middle school graduation requirements
   3. Advisor responsibilities vs. classroom teacher responsibilities
   4. E-portfolio directions: how to upload and manage
   5. Reflection
       i. Uniform questions across the curriculum
       ii. Sample reflections
III. Finished grade-level portfolios
IV. E-portfolio presentation: Defending your portfolio
   1. Do they look different in each grade? Does 6th grade have a smaller, less confrontational environment?
   2. Who is the audience?
   3. Who should be present?
       i. Portfolio team
       ii. Grade-level teachers (the ones responsible for creating the grade-level rubrics)
       iii. Parents (PTA? Or just parent of the child?)
       iv. Administrators

table of contents we created for our portfolio handbook when I was on the portfolio committee at my school.

Make sure you outline all the things you think folks will need to know. The handbook will be a living document that should be regularly revised based on the needs of your school. Remember to start with a shared vocabulary—really make sure that everyone has the same understanding of what important words mean. This common language will help mitigate any confusion when speaking about important aspects of the work. You all need to be on the same page, so working together to build a list of words and what they mean is a great place to start.

This journey is a long one. You won't be able to successfully implement the whole process as a school in one year's time, but an individual teacher who is trying to do this work alone could certainly move the needle on individual elements.

I encourage you to take the leap and implement student-led conferences and portfolios in your school or classroom. Kids are so much more than grades, and shifting away from the traditional processes that keep them compliant and ranked will markedly change how the whole culture thinks about learning. I can't wait to see what you come up with—and remember, I'm here to help if you need me. Just reach out.

Acknowledgments

No book is possible without the help of many. Thank you to the ASCD publishing team and the many educators who so willingly shared their stories with me in order to make a more authentic read for you. Each contributor helped to add depth to this book and I'm grateful for their generosity. Thank you to Bonnie Nieves, Lance Piantaggini, Jay Percell, Lisa Hicknell, Ro Tierno, Layton McCann, Barbara Kasomenakis, Isaac Wells, The Core Collaborative, Erin Quinn, Tara Vandertoorn, and Meredith Klein.

Throughout this process, I've been so lucky to have friends and colleagues read and provide the feedback I needed to make this work as good as it could be. So, to Emma Chiappetta, Katie Harrison, MaryAnn DeRosa, and Connie Hamilton—please know how much I appreciate you and your brilliance. I am better because I have you all in my life.

Last but not least, I want to acknowledge Alejandro Sosa and Georgia Douvres, my partners in crime on the portfolio committee. The three of us worked hard to make a consistent and meaningful experience for our students and colleagues based on the research we conducted together.

Appendixes

Appendix A
Blank Template for Unpacking Standards

_____ Grade/Course _____

Focus Standard(s) Clusters

Research the Standards		
Conceptual Understanding	Procedural Fluency	Application

Leverage Vertical Learning Progressions	
Prerequisite Knowledge and Skills	Accelerated Knowledge and Skills

Learning Intentions	
Essential Question/Goal(s)	Big Ideas

The Learning Process
Success Criteria/Learning Targets

Surface Criteria	Deep Criteria	Transfer Criteria
I can . . .	I can . . .	**Near Transfer:** I can . . . **Far Transfer:** I can . . .
Surface Learner Strategies	**Deep Learner Strategies**	**Transfer Learner Strategies**
• Jigsaw method • Integrating prior knowledge • Summarization • Mnemonics • Direct instruction • Record keeping • Notetaking • Asking "Who?" "What?" and "How?"	• Organizing and transforming notes • Identifying underlying similarities and differences • Classroom discussion • Reciprocal teaching • Concept mapping • Metacognitive strategy instruction • Self-questioning • Teacher questioning • Inquiry-based teaching • Simulations • Asking "How?" • Asking "Why?"	• Transforming conceptual knowledge • Organizing conceptual knowledge • Formal discussions • Problem-solving teaching • Reading and synthesizing across documents • Peer tutoring • Asking "Should?" "Where?" "When?" and "To what extent?"

Brainstorm Formative Tasks		
Surface Tasks for New Learning	**Impact Team Deep Tasks**	**Impact Team Transfer Tasks**
		Near Transfer: I can . . . **Far Transfer:** I can . . .

(*continued*)

Self-Regulation of Core Habits of Learning		
Academic Capacity	**Emotional Capacity**	**Social Capacity**
☐ Perseverance ☐ Questioning and problem posing ☐ Quality communication ☐ Thinking interdependently ☐ Metacognition ☐ Thinking flexibly ☐ Other	☐ Self-awareness ☐ Empathy ☐ Openness and vulnerability ☐ Patience ☐ Humility ☐ Compassion ☐ Other	☐ Listening to understand ☐ Thinking interdependently ☐ Openness and vulnerability ☐ Patience ☐ Precise communication ☐ Other
Resources and Strategies to Teach Standards		
Resources		**Page**
Citation:		

Source: Copyright 2023 The Core Collaborative. Used with permission.

Appendix B
Stoplight Rubrics

Opinion Writing Stoplight Rubric

Note: This rubric is appropriate for students in grades 3–6. It can be modified for younger or older students.

Success Criteria **I am working on improving my opinion writing.**	I need help.	I need more practice.	I can help a friend.
I started by introducing my topic or book.			
I stated an opinion clearly.			
I supplied reasons that support the opinion.			
I used linking words to connect the opinion and reasons (e.g., *because, and, also*).			
I ended with a concluding statement or section.			
I strengthened my writing as needed by revising and editing.			

I am proud of _____

_____

_____.

Next I want to work on _____

_____

_____.

Year-Long Conventions Stoplight Rubric

Note: Build together as you go; do not share this rubric with students all at once.

Success Criteria **I am working on writing clearly so my audience can read and understand what I am thinking.**	I need help.	I need more practice.	I can help a friend.
Capitalization			
I capitalize the first word of a sentence and the pronoun *I*. (**M**y friend and **I** sent the gift card.)			
I capitalize proper nouns including holidays and the names of specific people, places, and products. (**Y**ou and **D**ana can spend the card at **W**almart in **N**ew **Y**ork or anywhere else. **H**appy **V**alentine's **D**ay!)			
I capitalize appropriate words in titles. (***P****eer* ***P****ower:* ***U****nite,* ***L****earn, and* ***P****rosper*)			
Punctuation			
I use commas in addresses. (123 Digit Street, Apt. 4A, Numberton, NC 56789)			
I use commas in greetings and closings of letters. (Dear Class, Blah, blah, blah. Sincerely, Isaac)			
I can form and use contractions. (did not = did**n't**, she will = she**'ll**, will not = wo**n't**)			
I can form and use possessives. (teacher**s'** books, dog**'s** bone)			

Spelling			
I spell high-frequency words correctly. (**because**, **friend**, **their**)			
I spell suffixes correctly. (spill**ed**, smile**s**, kind**ness**, laugh**ing**)			
I use the spelling patterns and generalizations I have learned. (*I* before *E* except after *C* as in rec**ei**ve and when sounded as *A* as in n**ei**ghbor and w**ei**gh; **every s**yllab**le** h**as a vo**w**el**)			
I use reference materials such as my word wall, beginning dictionaries, and online searches as needed to check and correct spellings.			

I am proud of _____

_____

_____.

Next I want to work on _____

_____

_____.

Appendix C
Student Reflection and Goal-Setting Examples

5th Grade Student Reflection and Goal Setting: Example 1

Fall 2022

Name: *Student 1*

First-Quarter Reflection and Goal Setting

Steps

- ☐ In your Grade 5 folder, create a folder called "Q1 Conference."
  - ☐ Rename this document "[your first name] Q1 Student Reflection 2022.McCann."
  - ☐ Move it to your Q1 Conference folder.
  - ☐ Any work or evidence that you would like to share during the conference that is digital can be placed in the folder. It can be a digital assignment (link or copy of document) or a paper-pencil assignment.
- ☐ Fill out the reflection form below.
- ☐ Plan your conference script.
  - ☐ Rename it "[your first name] Student-Led Conference Script."
  - ☐ Place it in your Q1 Conference folder.

On a scale of 1–4, rate yourself for this quarter in the following core areas:

- 4 = I **consistently** meet expectations for understanding and use the skills, concepts, knowledge, and behaviors **competently**, **confidently**, and **independently.**
- 3 = I meet expectations for understanding and use the skills, concepts, knowledge, and behaviors most of the time with **minimal support from my teacher.**
- 2 = I am **beginning to meet** expectations for understanding and use the skills, concepts, knowledge, and behaviors. **Support from my teacher is still required most of the time.**
- 1 = I have not yet begun to display my skills and knowledge at this time.

Subject Area	Rating	Evidence/Explanation
Language Arts	3	Sometimes I can talk to my friends but most of the time I feel pretty good about the subject!
Science	4	I think I'm very good at this because I can focus while I work and get things done.
Social Studies	3	I think I can be very good at geography but to be honest I think I could do better with the African American stuff we do.
Math	4	I try my hardest in math and I have fun while doing so, and I also get very good grades in my opinion.
Tiger Pause	4	I am engaged in what I need to do and find time to do useful things if I have finished all the work.

On a scale of 1–4, rate yourself on the following approaches to learning:

- ◆ 4 = Independently
- ◆ 3 = With limited prompting
- ◆ 2 = With frequent prompting
- ◆ 1 = Rarely

Approaches to Learning	Rating	Evidence/Explanation
Communication Skills	4	I think I follow others' instructions pretty well and I don't interrupt people when they are talking unless we are at lunch and they are saying rude stuff and I interrupt them to change the topic.
Listens to and follows the information and directions of others	4	
Listens actively and respectfully while others speak	4	

(continued)

Self-Management Skills	3.7	I use my time wisely and organize my time to find time to do homework or work on an activity for school.
Uses time effectively and appropriately	4	
Takes responsibility for one's own actions	4	If I do something I will not blame someone else. I will be honest and say that it was not them and it was me.
Demonstrates patience	3	If I'm being honest, sometimes I can get a little impatient, but I would say for the most part I'm pretty good at [demonstrating patience]. Like, when we have the chairs, I will wait until my day to use them unless I ask and they let me use it for the time they are not.
Social Skills	3.3	I always feel bad for someone when they get hurt or if they are feeling sad, so when I spot sadness, I will try my best to cheer them up.
Practices empathy and care for others	4	
Learns cooperatively in a group (is courteous, shares, takes turns)	3	I respect others and their ideas and listen to their thoughts, and I also suggest thoughts of my own.
Advocates for one's own rights and needs	3	Sometimes I forget to say what I would like, but I know I could personally work on this skill.

Please answer the following questions in complete sentences:

1. What was your greatest success this quarter? Why? This can be in any subject, but it needs to be learning-related and specific.

   My greatest success this year is probably being able to get things done. I think I get homework done often and I can finish activities in school so I don't make it homework.

2. What was the most difficult subject for you this quarter? Why?

   I find geography hard because it is a bit difficult to memorize things, but when I work with a partner to help quiz me, I feel pretty good!

3. What do you like most about school this year? Why?

    I like that we have a funny but also kind classroom. I personally think that when kids in this classroom learn their mistakes they can grow from it and be kinder people.

4. What do you need to improve in the second quarter? Why?

    I need to improve on a little bit of everything if I'm being honest. I can be better at math and geography and putting my words through my thinking filter. I can also be better at making fair decisions and work on my problem solving, too.

In this section, you will need to think about goals. Come up with one for each area.

Academic Goals

Language Arts (Reading, Writing, Spelling)
Figuring out words from the other words in the sentence. And spelling errors.

Science
Making predictions, probably.

Social Studies
I could get better at the Native American stuff we work on and also get better at memorizing the geography.

Math
Memorizing my multiplication tables and getting better at asking questions.

Tiger Pause
Finding things that are useful to the class when I finish my work.

Approaches to Learning: Think about your communication, self-management, and social skills. What would you like to improve in the next quarter and why?

I would like to work on problem-solving skills and communication skills, too.

Final Assessment of the School Year

1. I give 5th grade a grade of <u>8</u> because . . .

   I give 5th grade a grade of 8 out of 10 because people will include me in activities and not care if I'm a girl or boy and also because most times I feel like there are so many things and games I can play I can't choose. But also, sometimes people can be rude or say mean things to others and I personally don't like that.

2. My suggestions for improving 5th grade are (be realistic!):

   My suggestion to improve 5th grade is more science projects like the marker one and the apple weight and the sewer maggots because I think that they let kids work together and have fun while thinking of hypotheses and experimenting. I also think that giving students reading time is a good idea because they can improve their reading skills and start getting creative ideas because of reading. It also helps getting away from technology but also having fun in a way. I'm not so strong on this one but I think we should let students go on nature walks like in the path behind the school or on the trail that is next to the school playground.

5th Grade Student Reflection and Goal Setting: Example 2

Fall 2022

Name: Student 2

First-Quarter Reflection and Goal Setting

Steps

☐ In your Grade 5 folder, create a folder called "Q1 Conference."
  ☐ Rename this document "[your first name] Q1 Student Reflection 2022.McCann."
  ☐ Move it to your Q1 Conference folder.
  ☐ Any work or evidence that you would like to share during the conference that is digital can be placed in the folder. It can be a digital assignment (link or copy of document) or a paper-pencil assignment.
☐ Fill out the reflection form below.
☐ Plan your conference script.
  ☐ Rename it "[your first name] Student-Led Conference Script."
  ☐ Place it in your Q1 Conference folder.

On a scale of 1–4, rate yourself for this quarter in the following core areas:

- 4 = I **consistently** meet expectations for understanding and use the skills, concepts, knowledge, and behaviors **competently, confidently,** and **independently.**
- 3 = I meet expectations for understanding and use the skills, concepts, knowledge, and behaviors most of the time with **minimal support from my teacher.**
- 2 = I am **beginning to meet** expectations for understanding and use the skills, concepts, knowledge, and behaviors. **Support from my teacher is still required most of the time.**
- 1 = I have not yet begun to display my skills and knowledge at this time.

Subject Area	Rating	Evidence/Explanation
English Language Arts	2.7	I turn in my work late a lot, and I'm trying to fix that. I also forget my homework folder sometimes and that really doesn't help. I wish I could do better. I am trying.

(continued)

Subject Area	Rating	Evidence/Explanation
Science	4	I think I'm doing better in science than ELA. It's a much bigger interest of mine. The biggest science thing we've done so far was probably the 7 Up and Mountain Dew with the raisins experiment. I was more curious, and I really enjoyed it.
Social Studies/ Geography	3.8	I actually really enjoy geography. I find it quite interesting and fun. I think I'm good at geography, but I needed a bit of online help and help from a classmate, too. But now I'm caught up and know a few extra rivers and lakes!
Math	3.5	I think that math-wise, I'm decent. I think I'm fairly good at math, but it's definitely not my favorite subject, though. But I try to have fun doing it, and sometimes it's not all that bad.
Tiger Pause	2.3	In Tiger Pause, I tend to get very distracted. I know that I should do better. I didn't give myself a 2 or a 1 because sometimes I do things like word study (I get behind on that sometimes) or math (I get behind here, too).

On a scale of 1–4, rate yourself on the following approaches to learning:

- 4 = Independently
- 3 = With limited prompting
- 2 = With frequent prompting
- 1 = Rarely

Approaches to Learning	Rating	Evidence/Explanation
Communication Skills	3	I think I am OK at this. Sometimes I need a reminder of what I'm supposed to be doing.
Listens to and follows the information and directions of others	3	Sometimes the person talks for too long and I get a little bored. Other than that, I'm good.
Listens actively and respectfully while others speak	3	

Approaches to Learning	Rating	Evidence/Explanation
Self-Management Skills	**3.5**	I turn in my things late sometimes. I'm doing my best to stop.
Uses time effectively and appropriately	3	I try to be a really honest but kind person. Sometimes I can't do it. But I am giving 100% honest scores.
Takes responsibility for own actions	4	
Demonstrates patience	3.5	I really do my best. I try to be patient, but some things and people really get on my nerves.
Social Skills	**3.7**	I try to show sympathy and empathy. There are times when instead I focus on myself, though.
Practices empathy and care for others	3.5	I am one of those people who wants to compromise when there is a disagreement. I think I'm good in group projects.
Learns cooperatively in a group: being courteous, sharing, taking turns	4	
Advocates for one's own rights and needs	3.5	I try to lend a hand to those in need. Sometimes I just don't, though.

Please answer the following questions in complete sentences:

1. What was your greatest success this quarter? Why? This can be in any subject, but it needs to be learning-related and specific.

   I think learning about geography was best for me because I found it the most interesting. I love learning about things like lakes, oceans, gulfs, rivers, maps . . . it's just so interesting. I also like science, particularly chemistry. It's exciting to mix different things to make something new. It also makes me feel magical, like a witch.

2. What was the most difficult subject for you this quarter? Why?

   Honestly, all the responsibilities (homework, unfinished projects) and my friends. Some kids were kind and caring, and some were most certainly NOT. My parents, especially my dad, say that I need to have a growth mindset. My mom gives me a lot of feedback and ideas when it comes to friends, too.

3. What do you like most about school this year? Why?

I think it's actually everything. I love this school, even though there are tough times, tough things, and tough people. I feel like a part of a huge community where I'm there for everyone and everyone is there for me.

4. What do you need to improve in the second quarter? Why?

I think I need to get better at all my responsibilities and get more work done. I need to take it more seriously.

In this section, you will need to think about goals. Come up with one for each area.

Academic Goals

Language Arts (Reading, Writing, Spelling)
Complete more in less time. Only have one project overdue. Max of overdue time: One day, unless sickness.

Science
Be more curious. Explore more answers.

Social Studies / Geography
Learn five more lakes, five more rivers, and five capitals.

Math
Take it more seriously. Try harder on homework.

Tiger Pause
Stop being so distracted. Focus on work.

Approaches to Learning: Think about your communication, self-management, and social skills. What would you like to improve in the next quarter and why?

For communication, I need to run some things in my filter and use the T.H.I.N.K. acronym before I talk. For self-management, I want to be able to think more about my actions and take my work more seriously. And finally, for my social skills, I want to think a little less about myself and a little more about others.

Final Assessment of the School Year

1. I give 5th grade a grade of <u>6</u> because . . .

   I don't love all the procedures, but I like 5th grade fine.

2. My suggestions for improving 5th grade are (be realistic!):

   More accountability for things we do right and wrong. That's it.

Source: Courtesy of Layton McCann. Used with permission.

Appendix D
Elementary Student-Led Conference
Prep Sheets

Student-Led Conference Prep Sheet Example

Presenter: Student 3   **Conference Date:** 11-1-21   **Teacher:** Ms. McCann

---

Step 1/Slide 1: Introductions (Welcome family and introduce all adults)

"_Momma and Daddy_, this is my teacher, Ms. McCann."

"Ms. McCann, this is/these are my family member(s), _Momma and Daddy_."

"Thank you for taking the time to come to my conference."

Step 2/Slide 2: State Purpose and Agenda of Conference

"This is an opportunity for me to share who I am as a learner."

"I'll begin by sharing some of my work. Then, we'll have some time to talk about the ways I've grown as a learner and set goals for the next few months."

"Finally, we'll give you a chance to give feedback and ask questions."

Step 3/Slide 3: Explain and Share Student Work

"Here are some pieces of work I want to share with you. I'll explain what I learned from doing this work, and what this work shows about me as a learner."

Student Notes: M word study, because it shows I'm good at vocabulary and I worked hard and concentrated.

Step 4/Slide 4: Explain and Share Reflections
"Here are some reflections I wrote about my progress in 5th grade so far, starting with what's going well in 5th grade."   Student Notes: I have learned new vocabulary, algebra, and most importantly how to be a better friend.

Step 5/Slide 5: Explain and Share Student Goals
"Here are some of the goals I have for myself between now and the end of the year. I'd like to talk through why I chose these goals and the support I need from all of you."   Student Notes: Be better at math and make new friends, and to do that I want to be less stressed out about it and feel confident.

Source: Courtesy of Layton McCann. Used with permission.

Student-Led Conference Prep Sheet Template

Presenter: _____   **Conference Date:** _____   **Teacher:** _____

Step 1/Slide 1: Introductions (Welcome family and introduce all adults)
"Mom/Dad/Aunt/Uncle, etc., this is my teacher _____." "_____, this is/these are my family member(s), _____." "Thank you for taking the time to come to my conference."

Step 2/Slide 2: State Purpose and Agenda of Conference
"This is an opportunity for me to share who I am as a learner." "I'll begin by sharing some of my work. Then, we'll have some time to talk about the ways I've grown as a learner and establish goals for the next few months." "Finally, we'll look at my grades so far and give you a chance to give feedback and ask questions."

Step 3/Slide 3: Explain and Share Student Work
"Here are some pieces of work I want to share with you. I'll explain what I learned from doing this work, and what this work shows about me as a learner." Student Notes:

Step 4/Slide 4: Explain and Share Reflections

"Here are some reflections I wrote about my progress in 5th grade so far."

Student Notes:

Step 5/Slide 5: Explain and Share Student Goals

"Here are some of the goals I have for myself between now and the end of the year. I'd like to talk through why I chose these goals and the support I need from all of you."

Student Notes:

Source: Courtesy of Layton McCann. Used with permission.

Appendix E
Portfolios and Student-Led Conference Needs Assessment

CLARITY AND ASSESSMENT PRACTICES	Not Yet	Sometimes	Always
Standards are explicitly taught and used in class.			
Students understand and can speak in the language of the standards to discuss their own learning.			
Success criteria help to inform mastery levels.			
Students help co-create success criteria.			
Student achievement is transparently shared with all stakeholders.			
All students know how they are doing in my class at all times.			
All students have multiple opportunities to show what they know.			
All students' social-emotional needs are considered in my assessment practices.			
Students are assessed in a variety of ways, not just through tests.			
My classroom is primarily a workshop-style class.			
Project-based learning drives instruction and student engagement.			
Formative assessment practices are used to determine instructional choices for all students.			
Portfolios are used as a way for students to track their own progress of learning.			

Use this space for notes and reflection:

PORTFOLIO KNOWLEDGE AND PRACTICES	Not Yet	Sometimes	Always
Student portfolios have a clear purpose.			
Students know the goals and purpose of the portfolios and can speak to them.			
Success criteria for the portfolios are communicated clearly and regularly.			
Students know what evidence to collect for portfolios.			
There is a dedicated space for students to collect evidence.			
Students are allowed to select what evidence goes into their portfolio.			
Students reflect on their chosen evidence to support their demonstration of what they know and can do as it aligns with success criteria.			
Regular opportunities to review progress in the portfolio are a part of classroom learning and reflection.			
Student portfolio reflections show a deep understanding of learning and can identify areas of learning to set future goals.			
Students can demonstrate transfer of learning through regular connection opportunities of evidence in their portfolios to skills and content learned earlier and in other classes.			
Structures are in place in class that keep the process really clear for student success.			
Portfolios are an integral part of our assessment process that allows for student voice and choice in demonstration of learning.			

Use this space for notes and reflection:

FEEDBACK PRACTICES	Not Yet	Sometimes	Always
I provide a variety of feedback daily:			
In writing			
Verbal			
Nonverbal			
Feedback is aligned with learning targets and/or co-constructed success criteria.			
All students receive feedback aligned with their core needs based on strong relationships.			
There is regularly an open dialogue/communication of learning through feedback.			
Time is made in class to confer with students regularly to discuss learning (in groups and/or independently).			
Data are collected and shared based on learning targets and/or class objectives.			
Students provide feedback:			
To peers			
To the teacher			
To the larger school community			
Students regularly participate in peer feedback workshops.			
Students are adept at providing both constructive and positive feedback.			

FEEDBACK PRACTICES	Not Yet	Sometimes	Always
Students are adept at receiving feedback.			
Students take actions based on the feedback received to improve learning.			

Reflect on your feedback practices as they align to portfolio processes:

STUDENT-LED CONFERENCES	Not Yet	Sometimes	Always
Students are involved in the assessment for learning process.			
Students can speak to their learning in an articulate way that aligns with content and skills in my class using academic language.			
Students have time in class to prepare for conferences.			
Preparation for conferences is scaffolded using a Google form or some other survey option.			
Students review their portfolios for progress to gather evidence for focused conferences.			
Data from student surveys help me develop clarifying questions prior to the conference.			
Student voice and progress drive the direction of the conference.			
Students are empowered to ask questions to advocate for their own learning.			
Students share how their feedback and tracked progress has helped lead to their success.			

(*continued*)

STUDENT-LED CONFERENCES	Not Yet	Sometimes	Always
Students can speak to their level of proficiency based on predetermined criteria/progressions.			
Students have evidence to support their assessment of their learning for major competencies.			
Structures are in place to save time.			
Structures are in place for students to do productive learning while conferences are happening in class.			

Use this space to reflect on this content and set goals:

Questions for further thought and reflection:

1. What are your biggest challenges around current assessment practices?

2. What do you hope to gain from learning more and implementing the formative assessment process in your classrooms?

3. How do your students like to engage with the learning?

4. What role do goal setting and reflection currently play in your classroom?

5. In what areas do you feel you need additional professional learning support to be successful with portfolios and student-led conferences?

Appendix F
Student Case Study: Barbara Kasomenakis, High School Senior

The following case study is the script one of my former students used as she gave an end-of-the-year slide presentation. As you read it, notice areas of strength and connection and how having a portfolio and regular conferences prepared her for this experience. Today, Barbara is a college graduate who teaches formerly incarcerated people at the Fortune Society.

Hello, everyone . . . you have all been chosen to listen to me speak for a certain amount of time, so lucky you. I guess I'll just start.

I know this portfolio should show my growth from freshman year to now, but I thought it would be interesting to start with the first paper I was assigned in English class when I started WJPS in the 6th grade. I plan on majoring in English, something aligned with literature or art, so I think this would be an appropriate place to start.

The paper is titled "Ms. Bernhardt Story October 2009." This assignment was mostly a creative paper given so Ms. Bernhardt could see our skills as writers coming in from elementary school. At this point, I had never read a book longer than 100 pages, and television was very influential. Detective shows in particular seemed to capture my attention, and you can see this in the excerpt I'm just about to show you . . . I haven't touched this paper since 2009. . . all errors in grammar and sentence structure are kept the way they were:

> I sat quietly crossing my fingers that help was coming. One big body came in. "What do you know you about your 30-year-old brother you little runt?" I felt like shattered glass. MY brother? MY brother Francis? That one? I haven't seen him for 5 years. "I thought he was killed in a car accident." I replied quietly. His face frightened me. There were blood stains on his hand and sweat patches allover his body. "Is that right?" he growled. "Well let's just see if you really think that." All of a sudden, a tall black silhouette came knocking on the door, anxious to come in.

Right, so, highly influenced by television. I didn't understand the subtleties of language and just tried to excite the senses as much as possible. For the most part, this was written in a stream-of-consciousness style, and an understanding of the writing process was nonexistent.

There was no pre-planning, drafting, revising, etc. I was not interested in practicality and readability in this story. There is no sense of time or logical progression. Also, grammatical rules were mostly ignored! However, I did show potential in a creative side which has, I think, stuck with me until now.

Let's move on to the start of high school now . . . 9th grade. You'll already begin to see some drastic improvements in my work, but I still need change.

The next assignment I'm about to show you is another English assignment. This one was more involved and required research to prove our argument of whether George Milton (a character from Steinbeck's *Of Mice and Men*) should be charged with first-degree murder for shooting his friend, Lennie Small. Here I'll show you my attempt at convincing "the jury," or Ms. Marks:

> Milton's acts were premeditated and selfish, and he betrayed someone he looked after. He persuaded others to comply with him, and he had known all along that something so severe like this would happen after all. . . . He intended to kill Small by ending his life in a way that may have been considered a mercy killing but was not. Small was not terminally ill, just misunderstood. Although Milton was Small's guardian, he does not have the right to decide when a life should end.

This part of my paper was the conclusion. As you can see, there is a more logical pattern to my sentences. My thoughts are complete for the most part, and my language is used more purposefully. However, there is a lack of rhythm to my sentences and stylistically, I still had not developed my own voice. I remember not being confident with this paper and when compared to everyone else's in the class, you couldn't tell it apart. Also, if you were to read the rest of the paper you can see that I ditched the idea of backing up my claim with research and just inserted my opinion whenever I could. I did not analyze Steinbeck's reasons for having Milton kill Lenny and simply relied on the gut feelings I had. The author's intent was not something I prioritized, and this ultimately hindered my ability to have a deeper understanding of the novel.

The next assignment I'll be showing you is taken from my Living Environment class (or Biology) with Ms. Douvres. The goal of this experiment was to see what percent of saltwater concentrate is best for hatching brine shrimp. This assignment reintroduced me to the concept of the control/experimental groups and independent and dependent variables. This, among many other concepts in science, is something I've struggled with. . . . I always bypassed the scientific method and either focused on minute details or skipped to the conclusion. I don't like to give excuses, but I can see how this need to create, as seen in my paper in the 6th grade, has hindered my ability to succeed in subjects like science or math.

Unlike science, art is not based on evidence, but on experience. Art is not confined to logic, it is an expression of feelings. And unlike science, art does not work with a hypothesis and does not need evidence . . . it is separate from science, but sometimes, there can be some overlaps. I have an example of this overlap in the next assignment I am about to show you.

In my 9th grade geometry class, we considered the term "conceptual art" and the role of math (geometry, fractions, permutations) in producing art. We first created a conceptual art piece by following a set of instructions used by the artist Sol LeWitt. Then, we designed two conceptual art plans using math concepts—one in two dimensions, and another in three.

Unfortunately, I don't have the project to show you now, but I could explain my findings: Sol LeWitt used lines, geometric solids, ratios, patterns, formulas, and permutations to create his modern structures and wall paintings. The ziggurat-style skyscraper had the greatest influence on LeWitt's Four-Sided Pyramid, a structure we based this in-class assignment on (the one pictured here). This structure is made of blocks stacked and stepped back in an orderly pattern and is based on the geometry of the pyramid. This digression from regents-based math allowed me to see how something I enjoy so much like art and something I thought was out of my reach like math could intertwine nicely.

Next is my 9th grade U.S. history class. Most of the work we did align with a regents curriculum. The picture here is an example of a problem we would be asked [to respond to in class involving analyzing political cartoons]. Looking at this political cartoon now, I can point out five ways to analyze it:

1. Recognize exaggeration. Artists will often exaggerate or distort certain elements of the drawing to make a point. Some commonly exaggerated pictures might include a character's facial features or other parts of the body.
2. Understand symbolism. An artist may use symbols as placeholders for ideas or themes.
3. Understand labeling. The cartoonist may label certain elements in the cartoon. This will help identify the different pictures and ideas in the cartoon. Labels are often paired with symbols.

4. Understand analogy. The cartoonist may compare two things that are not alike. This technique may be used if there is a complex topic or idea that is difficult to understand. By comparing it to something else, it can be easier for the reader to understand.

5. Recognize irony. An artist may use irony by using words or pictures to describe the opposite of what is, such as what should be. This is usually done with humorous effect.

Many of these skills I learned in past English classes have transferred over to a subject like history as well. I have learned to read critically, and I began to consider the question "Why is this point important?" This allowed me to push beyond mere description into ideas that are convincing and argumentative and defend a position. The answer is choice three, by the way.

Now on to the 10th grade!

Here is a screenshot of a group project I did with Alyssa, Leanna, and Demetri. At this point in the year, we were focusing on Galileo's involvement in the Scientific Revolution. This assignment acts as a good indication of how well I worked with groups in the past. Listening to others and not being trapped in my own head was at first a difficulty. My initial thoughts of being the "weak link" plagued me and my reclusive writing habits still were the most comfortable to me. Yet through collaboration among my peers, I was able to recognize that the creative thoughts we all shared could be illustrated in a way that did not cast a person off into one ascribed group. I was slowly becoming more comfortable in a group setting and this can especially be seen in this project.

Next is an assignment from my 10th grade chemistry class with Dr. B. In this assignment, I spoke about J.J. Thomson's cathode ray tube. Here is an excerpt from the essay:

> Thomson used what is called the cathode ray tube. It is made of a big tube of glass that can be thought of as a soda bottle. It is sealed all over, and the air is pumped out. There are two pieces of metal at the thinner end of the glass tube. Thomson connected these two pieces of metal to a power source. A ray shot from the first metal piece across the tube created a glowing spot at the other end of the tube. It hits a special coating on the inside of the glass tube. Thompson did not know what was going on at the time. As we now know, electrons from that first piece of metal were shooting out and were attracted to the second piece of metal (which has an opposite charge) and were shot all the way across the tube.

For the most part, chemistry was one subject I really struggled with. Chemistry is almost entirely abstract; you cannot see molecules with the naked eye. I needed to be able to visualize what I was learning to make it into something practical to me. I also had to be comfortable with math up through algebra to understand and work chemistry problems. Part of the reason I found chemistry so daunting is that I was learning (and relearning) math at the same time I was learning chemistry concepts. This topic, however, offered me plenty of visuals, which helped me better understand what a cathode ray tube is (a high-vacuum tube in which cathode rays—beams of electrons emitted from the cathode of a high-vacuum tube—produce a luminous image on a fluorescent screen, used chiefly in televisions and computer terminals).

Relating chemistry back to English, I was not familiar with writing a research-style paper, which explains my lack of formalities in my language . . . my sentences also seem very contrived, which further shows my discomfort with writing this type of paper.

The next subject I'd like to move on to is Algebra 2. Here is an example of some formulas we had to use throughout the year.

Memorization was yet another problem I had in classes involving math. I felt like memorizing ran counter to the whole object of understanding. I was able to eventually memorize formulas like these and rattle off a whole series of concepts and ideas, but when asked to explain these ideas, I would draw a blank. Although I won't be using much of the math I've learned in real life, this topic ran counter to that. Sequences and series play an important role in various aspects of our lives. They help us predict, evaluate, and monitor the outcome of a situation or event and help us a lot in decision making. Adopting these effective analytical tools and processes helps to make better technological products, invent life-saving drugs and medical instruments, and increase business profitability. This may not be relevant to my life just yet, but maybe it will be eventually!

Now let's move on to the 11th grade!

I'll start with English. This class, among others, was one of my favorites out of all my years in high school. Ms. Destefano allowed for so much freedom in her class, and she introduced me to a lot of literature that I still treasure. *The Picture of Dorian Gray* in particular was a piece of literature I really enjoyed, and I wrote an essay discussing aesthetic philosophy and the dangers it posed in *Dorian Gray*. I would have never thought before starting this class that I would be interested in Victorian literature or even be able to understand it. I thought, "How can I even consider reading literature without understanding the work through its historical context?" This type of reading requires an immersed kind of thinking, and slowly I began to dive into the many subtitles of language used by

Victorian authors and the culture surrounding them. This class helped me to discover a newfound love for reading.

My interest in history also extended in Global class, where I wrote a paper on Pol Pot and his involvement in the Communist Party of Kampuchea (kam puh chia). In my essay I tried to stress the importance of my thesis statement and give the essay a sense of completeness. Although I don't think I left a final impression on the reader, I tried to redirect my readers (by readers, I mean Mr. Thompson). At this point, I understood that I could not simply summarize and repeat things already mentioned in my essay. I tried to synthesize information and create a new meaning when writing.

OK, I'll move on to my 11th grade trigonometry class with Mr. Gardner. This is one of the first math classes I somewhat enjoyed and did relatively well in. Perhaps it was because the first half of the year was spent revisiting similar concepts learned in last year's class, but nevertheless, I felt more prepared. This solid foundation allowed me to apply many of these skills in my passive solar design project. Here's a slide summarizing that:

> Passive solar homes are designed to take advantage of local climates by maximizing the energy from the sun to heat and cool the home.

Next is 11th grade physics with Ms. Katz. My patience in this class always seemed to wear thin. We really didn't apply physics to real-life situations and just focused on memorizing formulas and understanding how to solve computations. Even though I had a better grasp on math at this point, I couldn't be engaged by the subject . . . it just seemed so dull to me. This ultimately hurt me in the end. I could've done a lot better in the class if I'd persevered through that disinterest.

Next, I will be showing you another subject I felt similarly to initially, but realized that understanding a subject doesn't always rely on the way a teacher presents their information . . . it also depends on the individual.

I will be moving on to the 12th grade now. . . . I'll start with my macroeconomics class. I think a familiar feeling all throughout high school shared by many is "if any of this really matters." I tended to side with "no," but macroeconomics proved to be one of the most practical classes I've taken. Firstly, it provides us with the tools to judge the performance of an economy as a whole. Macroeconomics is also useful to the government for formulating appropriate policies, and for any business firm, the knowledge of macro is necessary because the demand for many firms' products is a function of income. I really didn't think starting this class I would be engaged since a majority of it involved graphing and following strict economic policies and prescriptions. However, this was one of the first times the bigger issues like the 2009 financial crisis were addressed, something very relevant to the country we live in. Understanding why economic problems arose was important to me, and knowing how to solve these issues seems like significant knowledge to have:

Reasons why the 2009 financial crisis happened

1. Banks created too much money . . .
2. . . . and used this money to push up house prices and speculate on financial markets.
3. Eventually, the debts became unpayable.
4. This caused a financial crisis.
5. After the crisis, banks refused to lend, and the economy shrank.

Another subject I found to be very useful was my environmental science class with Mr. V. Learning about environmental issues that plague us in the modern day gave me a better understanding of what precautions we should take as a society to prevent any more harm to ourselves, and the earth.

Next, I'd like to talk about my experience in my precalculus class . . . applying knowledge from my physics course and past algebra classes allowed me to take on bigger-scale projects, like one that dealt with derivatives and continuity among functions.

I'd like to conclude with a class that has been special to me. It took a class like 12th grade English to diminish my negative feelings about school and to restore an excitement even for a person so jaded like myself. It was difficult to choose just one assignment, but I will go with my final research paper, one of the most strenuous papers I've ever written.

Reflecting now, I notice the improvements in my writing scale from large to small. Bigger improvements include organization and cohesion between paragraphs strengthening my transitions, while smaller improvements include the reinforcement of certain stylistic choices. My voice as a writer and student overall has taken a more concrete shape. Reflecting on my learning allows me to transform experience into genuine learning about individual values and goals about larger issues. I have learned to tackle topics that will never be answerable yet develop arguments that help get closer to finding a solution. I am still unsure about what the next few months will bring, but I know that I will be able to apply the skills acquired this year not only in a classroom setting but in life as well.

Ms. Schneider asked for a metaphor and here it is: a weathervane. They're put on the highest point of a building to show the direction of the wind. I think this translates to my life because starting college is supposed to be a high point of my life, but regarding the direction I am going in . . . I am not quite sure about that. That will change frequently, but I am up to the challenge.

Source: Courtesy of Barbara Kasomenakis. Used with permission.

References and Resources

Ainsworth, L. (2013). *Prioritizing the Common Core: Identifying the standards to emphasize the most.* Amsterdam University Press.

Almarode, J., & Vandas, K. (2018). *Clarity for learning: Five essential practices that empower students and teachers.* Corwin.

Ayalon, M., & Wilkie, K. J. (2020). Developing assessment literacy through approximations of practice: Exploring secondary mathematics pre-service teachers developing criteria for a rich quadratics task. *Teaching and Teacher Education, 89*(103011). https://research.monash.edu/en/publications/developing-assessment-literacy-through-approximations-of-practice

Barnes, M. (2015). *Assessment 3.0: Throw out your grade book and inspire learning.* Corwin.

Bloomberg, P. J., & Pitchford, B. (2016). *Leading impact teams: Building a culture of efficacy.* Corwin.

Bloomberg, P., Pitchford, B., & Vandas, K. (2019). *Peer power: Unite, learn, prosper, activate an assessment revolution.* Mimi & Todd Press.

Bloomberg, P. J., Vandas, K., & Twyman, I. (2022). *Amplify learner voice through culturally responsive and sustaining assessment.* Mimi & Todd Press.

Blum, S. D., & Kohn, A. (2020). *Ungrading: Why rating students undermines learning (and what to do instead).* West Virginia University Press.

Burt, R., & Morris, K. (2020, September 12). The complete guide to student digital portfolios. *CampusPress.* https://campuspress.com/student-digital-portfolios-guide

Chiappetta, E. (2021, April 20). 4 ways to encourage students to ask questions. *Edutopia.* www.edutopia.org/article/4-ways-encourage-students-ask-questions

Chiappetta, E. (2022). *Creating curious classrooms: The beauty of questions.* ConnectEDD.

Couros, G. (2017, June 30). *What does your digital portfolio show?* https://georgecouros.ca/blog/archives/7450

Couros, G. (2020, May 5). *7 important questions before implementing digital portfolios.* https://georgecouros.ca/blog/archives/11660

Cronin, A. (2016, July 8). Student-led conferences: Resources for educators. *Edutopia.* www.edutopia.org/blog/student-led-conferences-resources-ashley-cronin

Dean, C. B., Hubbell, E. R., Pitler, H., & Stone, B. (2012). *Classroom instruction that works: Research-based strategies for increasing student achievement* (2nd ed.). ASCD & McREL.

Edublogs. (n.d.). *Categories vs tags.* https://help.edublogs.org/categories-vs-tags

Edutopia. (2021, April 22). How student-led conferences center the learning journey. www.edutopia.org/video/how-student-led-conferences-center-learning-journey

EUfolio. (2015). *ePortfolio implementation guide for policymakers and practitioners.* https://eufolioresources.files.wordpress.com/2015/03/eportfolio-implementation-guide_en.pdf

Feldman, A., Kropf, A., & Alibrandi, M. (1996, April). *Making grades: How high school science teachers determine report card grades.* Paper presented at the Annual Meeting of the American Educational Research Association, New York.

Hamilton, C. (2019). *Hacking questions: 11 answers that create a culture of inquiry in your classroom (Hack Learning Series).* Times 10 Publications.

Hawe, E., Lightfoot, U., & Dixon, H. (2017). First-year students working with exemplars: Promoting self-efficacy, self-monitoring and self-regulation. *Journal of Further and Higher Education, 43*(1), 30–44.

Hendry, G. D., & Tomitch, M. (2013). Implementing an exemplar-based approach in an interaction design subject: Enhancing students' awareness of the need to be creative. *International Journal of Technology and Design Education, 24*(3), 337–348.

Hendry, G. D., White, P., & Herbert, C. (2016). Providing exemplar-based "Feedforward" before an assessment: The role of teacher explanation. *Active Learning in Higher Education, 17*(2), 99–109.

Hughes, J. (2008). Letting in the Trojan mouse: Using an eportfolio system to re-think pedagogy. *Hello! Where are you in the landscape of educational technology?* Proceedings of ASCILITE (Australasian Society for Computers in Learning in Tertiary Education) conference, Melbourne, Australia, 2008.

Liljedahl, P. (2020). *Building thinking classrooms in mathematics, grades K–12: 14 teaching practices for enhancing learning.* Corwin.

Marzano, R. J. (2006). *Classroom assessment and grading that work.* ASCD.

Morris, K., & Burt, R. (2020, September 12). The complete guide to student digital portfolios. *CampusPress.* https://campuspress.com/student-digital-portfolios-guide

Nilson, L. B. (2015). *Specifications grading: Restoring rigor, motivating students, and saving faculty time.* Stylus Publishing.

Office of Teaching & Learning, Utah Valley University. (n.d.). *Using exemplars in the classroom.* www.uvu.edu/otl/blog/exemplarsintheclassroom.html

Percell, J. C. (2014). The value of a pointless education. *Educational Leadership, 71*(4). www.ascd.org/el/articles/the-value-of-a-pointless-education

Sackstein, S. (2015a). *Hacking assessment: 10 ways to go gradeless in a traditional grades school.* Times 10 Publications.

Sackstein, S. (2015b). *Teaching students to self-assess: How do I help students reflect and grow as learners?* ASCD.

Sackstein, S. (2017). *Peer feedback in the classroom: Empowering students to be the experts.* ASCD.

Sackstein, S. (2021). *Assessing with respect: Everyday practices that meet students' social and emotional needs.* ASCD.

Sackstein, S., & Terwilliger, K. (2021). *Hacking learning centers in grades 6–12: How to design small-group instruction to foster active learning, shared leadership, and student accountability.* Times 10 Publications.

Sadler, D. R. (2005). Interpretations of criteria-based assessment and grading in higher education. *Assessment and Evaluation in Higher Education, 30*(2), 175–194.

Sadler, D. R. (2010). Beyond feedback: Developing student capability in complex appraisal. *Assessment & Evaluation in Higher Education, 35*(5), 535–550.

Schippers, M. C., Morisano, D., Locke, E. A., Scheepers, A. W. A., Latham, G. P., & de Jong, E. M. (2020, January). Writing about personal goals and plans regardless of goal type boosts academic performance. *Contemporary Educational Psychology, 60.*

Scoles, J., Huxham, M., & Mcarthur, J. (2012). No longer exempt from good practice: Using exemplars to close the feedback gap for exams. *Assessment & Evaluation in Higher Education, 38*(6), 631–645.

Wiggins, G. P., & McTighe, J. A. (2005). *Understanding by design.* ASCD.

Wormeli, R. (2006). *Fair isn't always equal: Assessing and grading in the differentiated classroom.* Stenhouse.

Zerwin, S. M. (2020). *Point-less: An English teacher's guide to more meaningful grading.* Heinemann.

Index

Note: The letter *f* following a page number denotes a figure.

About the Author

Starr Sackstein is the COO of Mastery Portfolio, an EdTech start-up, and a veteran educator. She started her teaching career at Far Rockaway High School in the early 2000s, eager to make a difference. Quickly learning to connect with students, she recognized the most important part of teaching: building relationships. She worked as the director of humanities for West Hempstead Public Schools in West Hempstead, New York, and completed her advanced leadership certification at SUNY–New Paltz. Before her leadership role, Sackstein was a UFT Teacher Center coordinator and ELA teacher at Long Island City High School in New York. She also spent nine years at World Journalism Preparatory School in Flushing, New York, as a high school English and journalism teacher, where her students ran the multimedia news outlet WJPSnews.com.

In 2011, the Dow Jones News Fund honored Sackstein as a Special Recognition Adviser, and in 2012, *Education Update* recognized her as an outstanding educator. In her last school-based position, Sackstein threw out grades, teaching students that learning isn't about numbers but about developing skills and articulating growth.

Sackstein is a National Board–Certified educator as well as certified as a Master Journalism Educator by the Journalism Education Association (JEA), for which she served as New York State Director from 2010 to 2016. She is the author or coauthor of many books, including but not limited to *From Teacher to Leader: Finding Your Way as a First-Time Leader Without Losing Your Mind*, *Teaching Mythology Exposed: Helping Teachers Create Visionary Classroom Perspective*, and *Peer Feedback in the Classroom: Empowering Students to Be the Experts*. You can learn more about all her published works on her Amazon page or her website, MsSackstein.com.

At speaking engagements around the world, Sackstein speaks about blogging, journalism education, bring your own device, and throwing out grades, which she also highlighted in a recent TEDx talk titled "A Recovering Perfectionist's Journey to Give Up Grades." In 2016, she was named one of ASCD's Emerging Leaders, and in 2022, she was included in the inaugural class of ASCD's Champions in Education. In recent years, Sackstein has spoken in Paris, Barcelona, India, Canada, Dubai, and South Korea on a variety of topics from assessment reform to technology-enhanced language instruction.

She began consulting full-time with the Core Collaborative in 2019, working with teams on assessment reform, and bringing student voice to the forefront of classroom learning. It is through her affiliation with the Core Collaborative that Sackstein became the publisher with Mimi and Todd Press, helping other authors share their voices around making an impact for students.

Balancing a busy career of writing and educating with being the mom of Logan is a challenging adventure. Seeing the world through his eyes reminds her why education needs to change for every child. Email her at mssackstein@gmail.com or follow her at www.twitter.com/MsSackstein.

Related Resources

At the time of publication, the following resources were available (ASCD stock numbers in parentheses).

Amplify Student Voices: Equitable Practices to Build Confidence in the Classroom by AnnMarie Baines, Diana Medina, and Caitlin Healy (#122061)

Assessing with Respect: Everyday Practices That Meet Students' Social and Emotional Needs by Starr Sackstein (#121023)

Classroom Assessment Essentials by Susan M. Brookhart (#124001)

Demonstrating Student Mastery with Digital Badges and Portfolios by David Niguidula (#119026)

Digital Portfolios in the Classroom: Showcasing and Assessing Student Work by Matt Renwick (#117005)

Fostering Student Voice (Quick Reference Guide) by Russ Quaglia and Kristine Fox (#QRG119034)

Giving Students a Say: Smarter Assessment Practices to Empower and Engage by Myron Dueck (#119013)

How to Look at Student Work to Uncover Student Thinking by Susan M. Brookhart and Alice Oakley (#122011)

Peer Feedback in the Classroom: Empowering Students to Be the Experts by Starr Sackstein (#117020)

The Power of Voice in Schools: Listening, Learning, and Leading Together by Russ Quaglia, Kristine Fox, Lisa Lande, and Deborah Young (#120021)

Teaching Students to Become Self-Determined Learners by Michael Wehmeyer and Yong Zhao (#119020)

Teaching Students to Self-Assess: How do I help students reflect and grow as learners? (ASCD Arias) by Starr Sackstein (#SF116025)

For up-to-date information about ASCD resources, go to www.ascd.org. You can search the complete archives of *Educational Leadership* at www.ascd.org/el.

ASCD myTeachSource®

Download resources from a professional learning platform with hundreds of research-based best practices and tools for your classroom at http://myteachsource.ascd.org/.

For more information, send an email to member@ascd.org; call 1-800-933-2723 or 703-578-9600; send a fax to 703-575-5400; or write to Information Services, ASCD, 2800 Shirlington Road, Suite 1001, Arlington, VA 22206 USA.

WHOLE CHILD
TENETS

1 HEALTHY
Each student enters school healthy and learns about and practices a healthy lifestyle.

2 SAFE
Each student learns in an environment that is physically and emotionally safe for students and adults.

3 ENGAGED
Each student is actively engaged in learning and is connected to the school and broader community.

4 SUPPORTED
Each student has access to personalized learning and is supported by qualified, caring adults.

5 CHALLENGED
Each student is challenged academically and prepared for success in college or further study and for employment and participation in a global environment.

The ASCD Whole Child approach is an effort to transition from a focus on narrowly defined academic achievement to one that promotes the long-term development and success of all children. Through this approach, ASCD supports educators, families, community members, and policymakers as they move from a vision about educating the whole child to sustainable, collaborative actions.

Student-Led Assessment relates to the **engaged, supported,** and **challenged** tenets.
For more about the ASCD Whole Child approach, visit **www.ascd.org/wholechild.**